THE DEVELOPING CHILD *edited by*
Jerome Bruner   Michael Cole   Barbara Lloyd

PUBLISHED
Mothering *Rudolph Schaffer*
Play *Catherine Garvey*
Distress and Comfort *Judy Dunn*
The Psychology of Childbirth *Aidan Macfarlane*
The Perceptual World of the Child *Tom Bower*
Children's Drawing *Jacqueline Goodnow*
The First Relationship *Daniel Stern*

FORTHCOMING
Memory *Ann Brown*
Perception and Attention *Jerome Bruner*
Learning Difficulties *Sylvia Farnham-Diggory*
Child Abuse *Henry Kempe*
Moral Development *Elliot Turiel*
Children's Growth *James Tanner*
Early Language *Jill and Peter de Villiers*
Learning to Talk *Katherine Nelson*

NICHOLAS TUCKER, the author of *What is a Child?*, is a former educational psychologist who is now a Lecturer in Developmental Psychology at the University of Sussex. He has written two previous books and numerous articles and reviews on the theme of children and their cultural environment, as well as producing four books for children themselves.

The editors of THE DEVELOPING CHILD

JEROME BRUNER helped found the Center for Cognitive Studies at Harvard in 1960, and served there as Director until 1972. He is currently Watts Professor of Psychology at the University of Oxford and Fellow of Wolfson College, Oxford. He has long been interested in the nature of perception, thought, learning, and language, and has published widely on these topics. At present he is focusing his research on the early development of language in infants and on the role of the pre-school in early child development.

MICHAEL COLE is Director of the Laboratory of Comparative Human Cognition, at the Rockefeller University in New York. Trained initially as a psychologist, his research in recent years has led him into the fields of anthropology and linguistics in an attempt to understand better the influence of different cultural institutions, especially formal schooling, on the development of children. He is editor of *Soviet Psychology*, and his most recent book, co-authored with Sylvia Scribner, is entitled *Culture and Thought*.

BARBARA LLOYD is Reader in Social Psychology at the University of Sussex, author of *Perception and Cognition: a Cross-Cultural Perspective*, and editor (with John Archer) of *Exploring Sex Differences*. Her interest in child development has always been strongly cross-cultural (her first research was published as part of the Whiting's *Six Cultures* study). She has recently investigated cognitive development among both English and Nigerian children.

WHAT IS A CHILD?

Nicholas Tucker

Open Books
London

First published in 1977 by Fontana/Open Books
and Open Books Publishing Limited,
11 Goodwin's Court, London WC2N 4LB

© Nicholas Tucker 1977

ISBN 0 7291 0006 5

A paperback edition of this book jointly published by
Fontana/Open Books is available from 14 St James's Place,
London SW1A 1PF.

Printed by Billing & Sons Ltd.,
Guildford, London and Worcester

Contents

Editors' preface

Recent decades have witnessed unprecedented advances in research in human development. Each book in *The Developing Child* reflects the importance of this research as a resource for enhancing children's well-being. It is the purpose of the series to make this resource available to that increasingly large number of people who are responsible for raising a new generation. We hope that these books will provide rich and useful information for parents, educators, child-care professionals, students of developmental psychology, and all others concerned with childhood.

JEROME BRUNER *University of Oxford*
MICHAEL COLE *The Rockefeller University*
BARBARA LLOYD *University of Sussex*

Preface and acknowledgements

'It is quite surprising to see the wickedness of young boys.'
Dr Thomas Arnold, Headmaster of Rugby School

'I ask parents to eliminate any need for redemption, by telling the child that he is born good – *not born bad*.'
A. S. Neill, Headmaster of Summerhill School

Disagreement over the nature of children is nothing new, and something by no means confined to schoolmasters. Disputes and expressions of faith have cropped up in almost identical forms throughout history. Sometimes they tell us as much about those who hold the opinions as they do about children themselves. For some, childhood is something that would be fine in itself if only we could stop interfering and let each child work things out for himself. As the most famous philosopher of this school, Jean-Jacques Rousseau, wrote in 1762: 'God makes all things good; man meddles with them and they become evil.'[1]* Latter-day followers continue to broadcast the message. John Holt, for example, has written recently, 'In important matters, nobody can know better than the child himself.' Children must have 'the rights, privileges, duties, responsibilities of adult citizens'.[2] These include the rights to consume tobacco, alcohol and drugs, and also the freedom to set up a business, and have sexual intercourse with whomsoever he or she chooses.

This is a position that might strike many contemporary parents as somewhat extreme, particularly those who are in

* Superior numerals indicate references on pp. 117–21.

some sense heirs to the puritan tradition in their attitudes to children. In this view, a child is born essentially flawed in character, and can only be controlled, and thus ultimately saved from himself, by a firm hand at home and elsewhere. Today, this type of attitude appears particularly often in discussions of children's education, and it underlies a deep distrust of the relaxed, child-centred methods of teaching current in many schools. A succession of *Black Papers* on education, recently published in Britain in an attempt to halt a suspected slide in school standards, have put this view forcefully. 'Children are not naturally good,' claims a recent edition. 'They need firm, tactful discipline from parents with clear standards.'[3] These words could have been written at almost any time in Western history.

The disagreement is absolutely fundamental; to resolve such opposite opinions to everyone's satisfaction would be to advance a view not just of the child but also of man with which everyone would feel able to agree – something that may always be extremely unlikely. However, it is possible to discover a number of universal truths about the nature of childhood, particularly in the areas of physical and intellectual growth, personality development and likely social experience. Of course, these universals may operate in very different cultural milieux – and anyone attempting to identify what is unique about childhood must try to find possible common factors in some otherwise utterly different social settings. Yet children are not completely formed in the image of the society they live in. There are certain essentially childish traits that transcend different cultures and climates.

As just one example, all young children tend to have trouble pronouncing certain sounds and words such as 'th', or 'dog' and 'sock', producing the lisps and other minor speech aberrations typical of beginners. At the same time, recent work on the development of language, notably by Daniel Slobin, has drawn attention to the common ways in which all children structure their early language. These observations provide some support for Noam Chomsky's hypothesis that children are born with a natural propensity to acquire language, a 'language acquisition device' that manifests itself in similar ways whatever the culture. All young children appear to have the ability to learn language, without any sort of formal tuition, even in quite deprived or discouraging circumstances. Moreover, in their early speech children tend to utter words and phrases entirely of their own creation – the very opposite of mere parroting. Thus an English-speaking child may produce plurals like 'mouses', verbal endings such as 'The cuckoo clock has goed', or sentences like 'Milk all-gone', all of which he himself appears to have constructed, following his own innate sense of language structure. By the age of three or so, it has been claimed, he may have mastered many of the essential grammatical structures necessary for the production of complex speech.

There remains a great deal of argument over how universal these early speech processes are, but most contemporary psychological research in this area supports the idea that small children everywhere structure speech according to certain common principles But as one would expect, wherever generalizations about human behaviour are concerned, there are always exceptions. 'Thank you, madam, the agony is abated' was the reply extracted from the four-year-old Thomas Macaulay, after an anxious inquiry from his hostess over a matter of spilt coffee on his legs.[4] His Victorian contemporary, Thomas Carlyle, who had not yet spoken in his first eleven months, amazed his household by asking suddenly one day, 'What ails wee Jock?', on hearing another child crying.[5]

But great men and unusual children apart, there can surely be some agreement on characteristic childish speech, especially if one is thinking of the earliest years. We can form a generalization about children that does seem to hold true across different cultures and eras. Where speech is concerned, most children manifest certain hesitations, habits and irregularities that are commonly termed 'childish', and there is ample evidence from the past that this has always been so: from Samuel Butler's novel *The Way of All Flesh*, for example, we recall the savage beating Ernest Pontifex received at the age of three for his persistent inability to pronounce 'come' as anything other than 'tum'.[6] Earlier than this, in France, Heroard, Louis XIII's doctor, records in his diary his charge's childish pronunciation of certain words: *vela* for *voilà*, *équivez* for *écrivez*, and so on.[7]

The task for this book, therefore, is to try to tease out any other characteristics common to all childhood, such as a particular form of linguistic development, that seem to exist whatever the culture. This is no easy matter; among the endlessly diverse cultures of different places and times, we find an almost equal diversity in the immature of our species and in the way they are treated. In Chapter 1 we will try to single out such differences; in Chapters 2, 3 and 4 we will look for the features of physical growth and psychological development that nevertheless impose some constraints within which these variations exist. These will indicate the extent to which we can answer our question: What is a child?

In order to avoid generalizing from children in our own society to all children everywhere else, we have to start from the very first principles. And a wide variety of disciplines can contribute data to our search – indeed must, since no one discipline could ever hope to cover all the facets of childhood.

I hope that this book may make readers reconsider what exactly they mean when using words, as we all do, like 'infantile', 'childish' and 'childlike'. Discussion about children, like so much recent discussion about women, very often carries political implications, whether admitted or not, in that it usually involves a vision of society, either as it is or as the writer thinks it ought to be. If we can identify factors which are common to all children, it will become easier to give these generalizations the scrutiny they deserve. In the past, history or religion have frequently been cited by the generalizers as supporting evidence; in this century it is often psychology that is used as justification for claims about 'the child'. There are good reasons for this: psychological studies have revolutionized – there is no better word – our understanding of children. One of the tasks of this book will be to explore the different claims psychologists have made about what children can do and how they behave.

I would like to acknowledge the help and stimulation I have

received from colleagues at the University of Sussex teaching with me on both the *Human growth and development* and the *Images of childhood* courses, and especially from John Sants, always so willing to listen to ideas and to share his own. No one other than myself, however, can be held responsible for the following text. May I also ask sensitive readers to forgive me for referring to the baby or the child as 'he' but never 'she'. This is not prejudice, I hope, but a matter of literary convention. In fact, as any developmental psychologist knows, baby girls on the whole develop more speedily than boys, and often maintain this ascendancy throughout childhood.

May I lastly thank the editor of *New Society* for allowing me to quote from the various articles I have written for him on this subject in the past, the University of Sussex for granting me leave in order to complete this work, and my wife, to whom this book is affectionately dedicated, for making things so comfortable at home while I wrote it.

1/Childhood in different cultures

IS THERE A 'NATURAL' COURSE OF CHILDHOOD?

'From the moment of birth, man's organismic development, and indeed a large part of his biological being as such, are subjected to continuing socially determined interference.'[1] In this sense, as Peter Berger and Thomas Luckmann go on to point out, 'Ways of becoming and being human are as numerous as man's cultures.' To the extent, therefore, that man constructs his own nature, we should expect to find marked variations in what passes for childhood in different societies. The human baby is born in an exceptionally undeveloped state, and progressively adapts himself to his particular environment. Later, he becomes more aware of the social pressures surrounding him. Factors that determine the nature of and variation between these pressures in different societies may be economic, geographical, historical and cultural.

Faced by such diversity, some ethologists have tried speculating about the nature of early man, the original hunter-gatherer, and about likely uniformities in his behaviour and the way he brought up his young. For example, in primitive bushmen societies today, which are thought to resemble original hunter-gatherer cultures, mothers are apt to suckle their babies very frequently, rather than to adopt spaced feeding, as in Western societies. Does this therefore prove that frequent suckling is a more natural process for human beings?

'Natural' is of course a term full of pitfalls in any discussion of human behaviour. Humans will adapt to the society in which they find themselves; what may be natural in one society may be highly inconvenient in another. Frequent suckling and later close contact may be suitable in a simple society, where the mother works at home and family ties remain paramount in later life. In a mobile, Western society, however, it may be important to accustom the baby to the occasional absence of his mother, who may need to go out to work or lead a life more independent of her children. Later, the child will be expected to leave home himself, and eventually sever the connections with the household. Child-rearing practices that have not helped prepare him for this type of breach may be inappropriate or even positively harmful.

'Natural' behaviour in this sense would seem to imply 'adaptable' behaviour, and children have an undeniable capacity to adapt to very different circumstances. This adaptability is one key to the way in which universals of childhood become transformed by different social conditions. Studying children in one environment, therefore, may not necessarily act as an efficient guide to how they function in another. But while acknowledging this essential variability, it is still fair to ask whether all mankind has inherited certain ways of behaving which were once suitable for life in a hunter-gatherer society. That kind of society, in the comparatively brief time man has been on this planet, has after all made up some 90 per cent of the total human experience.

Ethologists believe that mankind still exhibits unmistakable signs of his common pre-agricultural past, in for instance certain universal techniques for non-verbal communication, in common patterns of attachment between mother and child, and in the persistence of apparently worldwide behavioural similarities, especially among the young, such as various forms of play. But whatever the significance of such inborn mechanisms, in themselves a matter for considerable argument, it is also true that only man has the ability to pass on accumulated knowledge and social attitudes to his offspring, implementing what Julian Huxley calls a type of cultural evolution. Quite apart from his genetic inheritance, every human at some stage must also acquaint himself with 'what everyone knows' about his society, the 'assemblage of maxims,

morals . . . values, beliefs, myths'.[2] The extent to which childhood can be defined as an imperfect or immature appreciation
of this sort of institutional order will be the question for the
rest of this chapter.

HAS CHILDHOOD ALWAYS EXISTED?

Historical evidence is crucial in any consideration of childhood universals, because it reveals repeated patterns, and also
because it shows the huge differences in the way children were
treated and expected to behave at different periods. Cross-
cultural studies, too, can highlight these kinds of contrast.
There is plenty of research on children from other countries,
which by suggesting links between all youthful behaviour may
help build a true concept of the child. This type of cross-
cultural psychology has revealed close parallels all over the
world between the onset and growth of childhood skills. However, the method is sometimes less useful for more subtle
comparisons. When it comes to describing intelligence and
general habits of thought, for example, the tests that are helpful in one society may not be relevant in another, and attempts
to devise 'culture-free' tests have been disappointing except
at a rather unsophisticated level. There are also numerous
studies now available of higher mammals other than man,
which may also be useful when we are looking for universal
needs and behaviour in areas such as attachment, fear or play.
A distinguished psychologist in this area, Harry Harlow, has
frequently pointed out such analogies: children's behaviour
at a second-grade school picnic, for example, reminds him
irresistibly of the play activities of young monkeys (a thought
that might occasionally have occurred to the organizers of such
events too). There is always the problem, when drawing this
type of parallel, of reconciling the differences between human
beings and other higher mammals with the similarities that
may also be evident. But such studies may usefully amplify
certain concepts of childhood.

One of the most radical historical studies of the child is
Philippe Ariès's *Centuries of Childhood*, which suggests that

childhood as we know it now is something largely invented in the last 300 years. Before that, he claims, adults and children were barely distinguishable; they shared similar leisure activities and frequently the same type of work. Ariès's study can stand as a good example of the strength and weakness of the historical position. Some historical findings must affect our view of the child: the fact, for example, that children of three were once expected to work at certain cottage industries is relevant to any consideration of the very young child's potential. One inevitable weakness, though, is that a historian can only generalize from the sometimes limited evidence available. In Ariès's case, there were many records he could draw upon for the upbringing of the Dauphin, later Louis XIII. But when it comes to detailing the lives of the vast majority of children who do not figure in written accounts or in the reminiscences of contemporaries, then any historian is in trouble. Evidence that exists on day-to-day life in the home quickly grows more meagre the further back one goes in history. How many mothers or nurses, for example, have left accounts of their experiences with the very young? History tends to be male-oriented; very often it is fathers and, later on, teachers who have provided us with what historical evidence we have about the behaviour of children, and then it is usually in describing a remarkable child or in advancing a particular piece of educational propaganda. It is not altogether surprising that Ariès has sometimes been criticized for constructing his theory too much around a tiny, unrepresentative section of French society.

Even accounts of the better publicized childhoods of the great can be very sketchy and biased in their selection of facts. 'Biographers and autobiographers in the seventeenth and eighteenth centuries either ignored the childhood of their subjects or treated the events of childhood simply as indications of later development. The focus was more on remarkable instances – close scrapes with death, providential good fortune, and the like – than on organic growth.'[3] This situation improved by the nineteenth century; yet even the 'baby biographies' (including Darwin's *A Biographical Sketch of an*

Infant) that began to appear, covering some of the unexceptional events of childhood, tended to rely upon irregular observations, often using the child as a mere prop for some particular theory of development and so viewing his behaviour very selectively. In Darwin's case, despite the brilliance of some of his observations, he tended to view his child as something of a living expression of the theory of evolution, duly recapitulating early human history in the progress of his development. G. Stanley Hall, one of the pioneers of developmental psychology in the United States, was probably the first psychologist to use anything resembling modern research approaches. Yet when he tried to collect reliable evidence that might have been useful for us to look back on today – such as a collation of the heights and weights of American schoolchildren towards the end of the nineteenth century – he found it difficult to obtain accurate records. Parents in some cases refused permission for such basic research on their children.

Even when comprehensive records do exist, a historian can rarely take them at face value. For one brief example, let us look at child coalminers in nineteenth-century Britain. The facts, as they emerge from early official inquiries, make depressing reading. Such work, in such conditions, would surely be considered by most to be inimical to any child, a violation of childhood. It may therefore come as some surprise to find a witness to the contrary: 'We had to cut the timber and put the props up. We *did enjoy* life down the mine. You had to keep fit.'[4] So wrote John Thomas Limbert, a miner's son born in 1885 who went down the mines at thirteen or fourteen years old. Another miner's son, Jack Lawson – born four years before – writes rather less affectionately about the 'dark prison below', where he had to spend ten hours a day at work.[5]

What does such comment tell us? Limbert went down the mines some fifty years after reports from the Royal Commission had drawn public attention to the disgusting working conditions for children. Perhaps he was looking back in nostalgia, leaving it to the politically aware Jack Lawson, later to become a socialist member of parliament, to remember more accurately the 'great, cold, gloomy shed, with the prospect of ten hours spent in dim passages and tunnels of rock and coal thousands of feet below'.[6] Would Limbert have felt differently if he had started work much younger, or was he always an unusually cheerful person whose comments cannot represent those of a whole generation of youthful coalminers? Historians, then, can answer general questions on such topics as changing conditions in the mines, but those involving individuals – Limbert himself, and how typical his feelings or Jack Lawson's were at the time – cause more difficulty.

To return to Ariès, and our search for childhood universals: the term 'childhood' seems for Ariès to relate to differences in knowledge and social behaviour between adults and children. In a complex society, these are chiefly recognized within specific social institutions such as schooling or apprenticeship that are necessary for the education of the young in a post-agricultural economy. In less complex societies, he argues, children are simply treated as small adults, and they are not seen to need any particular education or protection. Thus,

> In medieval society the idea of childhood did not exist; this is not to suggest that children were neglected, forsaken or despised. The idea of childhood is not to be confused with affection for children: it corresponds to an awareness of the particular nature of childhood, that particular nature which distinguishes the child from the adult, even the young adult. In medieval society, this awareness was lacking.[7]

Accordingly, children and adults might wear the same clothes, share the same simple work, and also leisure pursuits – with everyone joining in rustic games on feast days. In the same way, there would be little concern with chronological age as such; many people would neither know nor care how old they or their children might be, at a time when the exact recording of dates of birth was something of a rarity.

By the end of the seventeenth century, Ariès goes on, children began to wear distinctive clothing. At the same time, the growing importance accorded to education could only emphasize the differences in knowledge and attainments between educated adults and their offspring. Fewer children simply modelled themselves upon their parents in work or play. With the rise of the professional classes, work itself became an altogether more mysterious, abstruse matter – children of such parents might start preparing themselves for future work roles by abstract learning at school in company with their peers. At home, they might also be increasingly excluded from adult life, with their own rooms, bedtimes and eventually their own different types of food and drink. At the same time, adults started to regard their children rather differently, taking a more obvious and affectionate interest in them. In this way, the child as miniature adult gradually gives way to the child that we can all recognize today.

Ariès can only draw upon the evidence available to him, and his picture of the evolution of childhood is biased towards literate homes and the diaries, letters and pictures concerning children that have been found in them. But he himself believes that in the home of the poor peasant during the sixteenth and seventeenth centuries, or even in parts of the underdeveloped world today, many of the things he writes about in medieval France, before the development of the idea of childhood, would still apply. What is not always clear in his argument, however, is whether children were once seen as mini-adults by everyone (even their mothers) or simply by the male adults mostly responsible for the surviving historical evidence.

For example, all small children make demands that have to be met if they are to survive; treating them as young adults at this stage could hardly be less appropriate. In a sense, Ariès concedes this when he writes that 'as soon as the child could live without the constant solicitude of his mother, his nanny or his cradle-rocker, he belonged to adult society'.[8] But elsewhere he seems less than clear about the particular point at which a growing child would cease to need maternal or other special attention in this way. Certainly, there is a dismissive spirit in some medieval descriptions of children under seven. At a time of high infant mortality, adults in general may have felt more detached about the young, whose continued survival was always so much a matter of chance. But detachment, or as Ariès puts it a type of indifference to the idea of childhood in medieval society, does not necessarily imply ignorance or lack of recognition of some of childhood's basic characteristics. A society might be less aware of some of the physical, emotional and intellectual differences between adults and children – particularly the male adults, who would probably have a more distant relationship with the young anyway. But mothers would certainly know that young children were markedly dissimilar from adults in many ways, and the realization that the age of seven does in fact constitute some sort of important stage in development seems to have been a common enough concept in the past: it is 'the age usually given in the moralistic and pedagogic literature of the seventeenth century as the age for starting school or starting work'.[9]

In a largely agricultural society, where adults and children shared some of the same work and leisure pursuits, there might indeed have been fewer demonstrable differences, but even so it is possible to exaggerate the common ground that existed. Ariès makes a great deal of the fact that even up to the eighteenth century 'games' and 'play' did not suggest anything essentially childish. Children often took part in exactly the same activities as adults, whether it was singing, dancing, blind man's bluff, leapfrog, hide and seek, or even gambling at cards. Fairy tales, narrated by professional storytellers, again had an audience of adults and children.

There are still areas of common participation between the generations today, whether in beach games or watching television. Ariès is correct to draw attention to the much greater sharing of games in the past, but it seems likely that essentially childish play, in which adults had little or no part, also persisted. This is difficult to prove: children more rarely even than nursing mothers leave any historical records of their activities behind them. But from what is known about the development of the young we can predict that active, well-nourished children in any society will show certain characteristic patterns of essentially childish play.

Susanna Millar wrote recently:

There are several reasons why boisterous play should occur more in the young than in older animals. For instance, movements are less integrated and controlled in young mammals, and changes in the pattern of stimulation are likely to set off diffuse reactions more often than in the adult . . . The 'need' to move, jump, shout and 'let off steam' generally recognized in the young is not, however, merely a reaction to exciting stimulation although the latter may be an occasion for it. The fact that children find it less easy than adults to sit still for long periods, not to bang their heels against the chair, not to jump up, or move their arms, or touch objects, to execute fine movements with their fingers and modulate their voices, is not a question of having more energy to spill, but of comparative lack of integration and control of the movement systems.[10]

In other words the boisterous, spontaneous play so characteristic of the young seems to have a physiological basis, and so be something altogether less likely to occur in adults, except at odd moments. Its special, childish characteristics are well described by a seventeenth-century observer, the French philosopher Fénelon, who seemed to have no difficulty in distinguishing children's from adults' play. 'The (games) they like best are those in which the body is in motion. So long as they can be continually moving from place to place they are happy; a shuttlecock or a ball is all that is needed.'[11] It seems unlikely that most adults would readily join in these activities, or indeed play at other childish games. When Lorenzo de Medici played with his own young children, Machiavelli rather sniffily considered that behaviour inconsistent with what is expected from a head of state: 'It is possible he found more pleasure in the company of droll and witty men than became a man in his position, and he would often be found playing among his children as if he were still a child.'[12]

Perhaps the same exclusiveness to children can be claimed for most games that take place with or alongside others, and which account for much play among the young of higher mammals. These range from early games of physical contact with others to structured games involving whole groups. With children, some chants, customs and semi-rituals that occur in popular group games can be traced back as far as 500 years, and may date from even earlier. In this way, children hand down a type of indigenous play culture to succeeding generations; typically, adults forget about such games in maturity, and indeed this type of social play declines sharply at the onset of puberty. Of course, adolescents and adults may continue to play team games of various sorts, but these activities will now be more strictly rule-governed: 'games', rather than more spontaneous 'play'. It is the quality of spontaneity that is such a characteristic of children's games, both in the way they start, sometimes quite suddenly, and the way they can abruptly fade into some other activity.

We may agree with Ariès, therefore, when he states that 'in the early seventeenth century there was not such a strict division as there is today between children's games and those played by adults'.[13] But what follows seems needlessly exaggerated: 'Young and old played the same games.' 'In 1600 the specialization of games and pastimes did not extend beyond infancy; after the age of three or four it decreased and disappeared. From then on the child played the same games as the adult, either with other children or with adults.'[14] Overlap is not the same as convergence; everything we know about the psychology and physiology of children's play, especially when we see it on a continuum with the play we find in the young of other higher mammals, would lead one to doubt Ariès's last generalizations. In a crude sense, children are likely to show certain childhood traits in some broad areas *whatever* the culture. To ignore this and treat children simply as products of adult social expectations is bound eventually to lead to oversimplifications of this sort.

At another point, Ariès states that 'Language did not give the word "child" the restricted meaning we give it today: people said "child" much as we say "lad" in everyday speech. The absence of definition extended to every sort of social activity: games, crafts, arms.'[15] So far as these last two are concerned, physical and intellectual limitations would still surely affect the sort of work a child would be able to do, suggesting that some essential differences between children and adults would probably have been recognized in this area too. There are fairly frequent references by employers in the past to the fact that children could not always be relied upon to get on with their work without close supervision. As one nineteenth-century farmer complained, 'One boy is a boy, two boys is half a boy, and three boys is no boy at all.'[16] From Africa, in our own times, we can hear a rather similar story. Camara Laye was born in 1924 and brought up in a small village in French Guinea, where everyone worked at the fairly simple, primarily agricultural economy. In his fine autobiography, he describes his juvenile experiences of bird-scaring, a typical child's occupation in many rural communities.

> Everywhere there were to be seen these platforms mounted on forked stakes that looked as if they were riding the great flowing seas of the harvest fields. With my little playmates I would climb the ladder to one of them and scare the birds, and sometimes the monkeys that came to raid our fields. At any rate, that is what we were supposed to do, and we did it without grumbling, for it was more of a pleasure than a duty. But it sometimes happened that we became absorbed in other games, and forgot why we were there.[17]

TREATING CHILDREN AS ADULTS

Obviously, this sort of inattention need not only apply to children left on their own. Adult workers in similar situations may also not get on with the job occasionally but usually for different reasons unconnected with 'play' as such. In factory work or cottage industry, both children and adults would be expected to work long, arduous hours, sometimes at a constant speed dictated by a machine. Some of the accidents that happened to children in this sort of work may have arisen not from fatigue, but from the sheer monotony of the work, even less suited to the intermittent concentration and volatile spirits of a child. Of course, many children had to support themselves, and sometimes their parents too, by this sort of work. Daniel Defoe quotes one of the 'chief Manufacturers' in eighteenth-century Taunton as saying 'That there was not a Child in the Town, or in the Villages round it, of above five Years old, but, if it was not neglected by its Parents, and untaught, could earn its own Bread.'[18]

It is interesting to note that Defoe equates parental neglect with a child who has not been taught to work a loom and attain some sort of self-sufficiency. Even younger children were sometimes employed in cottage industries, working hours frequently inconceivable in a developed country today. But if small children managed such tasks, it was usually under the pressure of harsh discipline or appalling poverty. Few observers at the time ever suggested that such children looked particularly suited to this drudgery; it was more common to draw attention to their pinched, elderly appearance and their lack of spontaneity. So while there can be no argument that children, even small ones, were capable of performing arduous, boring manual tasks for hours on end in company with adults, it seems probable that they performed less efficiently, and sometimes at considerable cost to themselves, certainly in terms of their physical development, and possibly in other less tangible ways as well.

A child may be able to fit quite well into other adult social contexts, provided that not too many unexpected or over-ambitious demands are made of him. One would expect the child of a simple society, where individuals share many of the same beliefs, to learn the structure of his society more easily than he could in a complex, developed economy, with the kind of cultural richness and diversity that takes time and skill to understand. Simple societies should not necessarily be equated with primitive cultures; complex, diversified societies, with elaborate religions and codes of conduct, can exist at all levels of material progress. But those cultures, including our own, that are rich in nuances of social distinction, taboo or non-taboo topics for conversation, acceptable and unacceptable behaviour, contrasting philosophies, religions and politics, and all other subtle gradations and qualifications of belief and activity, cannot be mastered without time and a certain amount of trial-and-error learning.

To this extent, behaviour called 'childlike' may often simply describe an inability to cope with complex social expectations, the consequence of inexperience and lack of necessary understanding. Obviously, anyone in this situation may behave in such a way; it does not necessarily have to be a child. Many of the nineteenth-century jokes and cartoons that illustrate children's lack of social sophistication are repeated at the expense of servants and other 'social inferiors' too. In fact, servants in the past have often been treated rather like children, and regarded as individuals with a great deal to learn when it comes to 'proper' conduct in the presence of their masters. Books written especially to teach servants appropriate manners were termed 'babee's books' at certain times in history, and English puritans were often exhorted by their spiritual leaders to teach their servants to read – in very much the same terms as one would use for children.

TREATING ADULTS AS CHILDREN

All individuals kept at a lowly level, perpetually under the paternal supervision of an adult, may end up being treated like children. The American slave, for example, was often pictured as a natural companion for children, sharing some of their simple pleasures and fears, such as believing in ghosts or a host of other minor superstitions. Petty delinquencies, such as eating unripe watermelons, and their retribution, might be considered on a par with children's natural naughtiness. This caricature of the slave often found in the fiction of the time may be very far from the truth, but if adults in authority believe that others, whether young or old, are only capable of limited, simple expression and make sure they are treated accordingly, then to some extent those others may find themselves forced to act in this manner. When an uneducated servant or slave is addressed simply by his Christian name, or called 'boy', and master or mistress retain the right to inflict corporal punishment on him (which they did until comparatively recently, not least in British history), then he may not develop the type of personal autonomy that is part of what differentiates child from adult. In seventeenth-century Britain the term 'servant' might cover a variety of individuals, from farm worker to resident domestic staff, so this sort of authoritarian patronage must have affected a great many people. It persisted late into the nineteenth century, when servants could still be scolded for their 'unsuitable' boyfriends or clothes, and the cottages in some villages were inspected for orderliness and hygiene by the lord or lady of the manor as of right.

There is no doubt, therefore, that adults in authority can to some extent impose their conceptions of childishness both on children and sometimes on other adults too. In this sense the whole concept of childhood could be said to be a man-made phenomenon. Thus childhood may be lengthened and prolonged at some periods of history, and abbreviated at others, according to adult perceptions, needs and expectations. Writing about the British working class at the end of the nineteenth century, Paul Thompson states that 'parents, anxious to secure an economic return from their children's first wage-earning years at work, used various devices to postpone their marriage and setting up of their own homes'.[19] While dependent on the parental household, young people might still be told when to go to bed, and before what time they must return in the evenings, even when they were well over the age of twenty-one. Apprentices were often treated in the same semi-infantile manner; the young smiths in the forge at Candleford Green, writes Flora Thompson, ate at the foot of the table in silence. When their mistress was absent, there would be more freedom, but on one occasion, when

> someone rapped loudly upon the table with a teacup and said . . . 'Another pint, please, landlady!' the office door opened and a voice as severe as that of a schoolmistress admonishing her class called for 'Less noise there, please!' None of them resented being spoken to like children, nor did the young journeymen resent being placed below the salt . . . To them these things were all part of an established order.[20]

GAINING EXPERIENCE,
MAKING MISTAKES

Even so, while any individual can be kept back or indeed hastened on in his social development by the surroundings in which he lives, there are some limits to the speed at which most children can become socialized into adult ways, even when their society does not present a bewildering constellation of differing social attitudes, expectations and philosophies. One can quote again from Camara Laye's experience. In his village, children seemed to take quite a full part in some adult work and leisure pursuits from an early age, but throughout his autobiography he still describes moments which might have parallels in any childhood. At the age of six, for example, he sees a snake 'taking a turn' round the hut.

> After a moment I went over to him. I had taken in my hand a reed that was lying in the yard – there were always some lying around; they used to get broken off the fence of plaited reeds that marked the boundary of our compound – and I thrust this reed into the reptile's mouth. The snake did not try to get away: he was slowly swallowing the reed, he was devouring it, I thought, as if it were some delicious prey, his eyes glittering with voluptuous bliss; and inch by inch his head was drawing nearer to my hand. At last the reed was almost entirely swallowed up, and the snake's jaws were terribly close to my fingers.
>
> I was laughing, I had not the slightest fear, and now I know that the snake would not have hesitated much longer before burying his fangs in my fingers if, at that moment, Damany, one of the apprentices, had not come out of the workshop. The apprentice shouted to my father, and almost at once I felt myself lifted off my feet: I was safe in the arms of one of my father's friends![21]

Moments of danger in a child's life such as this are an inevitable product of lack of forethought and experience, one reason why the young of higher mammals need prolonged protection during their early stages. Adults in unfamiliar circumstances may also occasionally put themselves in great danger inadvertently, but they have had the time and the skills to master most of their environment, whereas for a child the home environment must initially be something new that he has to explore and learn about bit by bit. Camara Laye, after his initial dangerous encounter, learned the lesson that he was forbidden to play with snakes. But

> One day, however, I noticed a little black snake with a strikingly marked body that was proceeding leisurely in the direction of the workshop. I ran to warn my mother, as usual. But as soon as my mother saw the black snake she said to me gravely:
>
> 'My son, this one must not be killed: he is not as other snakes, and he will not harm you; you must never interfere with him.'
>
> Everyone in our compound knew that this snake must not be killed; excepting myself, and, I suppose, my little playmates, who were still just ignorant children.
>
> 'This snake,' my mother added, 'is your father's guiding spirit.'[22]

This is a good illustration of the task facing any child, even in a so-called simple society. He learns how to react to snakes from experience, only to discover later that things are more complicated than this: there are snakes and snakes. Any child, in any society, is always faced by this need to master the complexities of adult social conventions and structure. The more complex the environment, the longer it will take him to organize those sections of it he is expected to understand, as an adult, into manageable proportions. At the same time, the child – unlike the adult – is handicapped in this task, though increasingly less so as he grows older, by his intermittent concentration and intellectual limitations: 'I was still very young and was often able to forget myself in the moment; everything that passed through my head – and that was a great deal – was almost always fleeting and less enduring than the clouds that moved across the summer sky.'[23]

While he is still at the stage of learning to manage and understand his environment, a child may be more easily baffled or confused than an adult would be. One sad example of this is provided by the life of Robert Blincoe, an orphan born at the turn of the eighteenth century and reared in a workhouse. A cotton-mill owner applied to the workhouse for some new apprentices, and the children selected for him were heartlessly deceived about their future, being made to believe 'that they were all, when they arrived at the cotton-mill, to be transformed into Ladies and Gentlemen; that they would be fed on roast beef and plum-pudding, be allowed to ride their masters' horses and have silver watches and plenty of cash in their pockets'.[24] Believing all this, the children 'strutted about like so many dwarfish and silly Kings and Queens in a mock tragedy'. The reality, when they arrived at the mill, was watery porridge, black bread and discipline kept by a large man brandishing a horsewhip.

It is not difficult to find some equally unpleasant examples of adults being cheated in this way: Jews on their journeys to Nazi concentration camps were sometimes consoled with similar unreal fantasies, even up to the very last moment, when appearances could hardly be more to the contrary. In an atmosphere of fear, and far from a familiar environment, all human beings are prone to trust rumour and baseless speculation. On their home ground, however, most adults should have a certain basis of experience and knowledge – Freud's 'reality principle' – that makes them less susceptible to the tall story or the confidence trickster, although no human being can ever be completely immune from this sort of beguilement. Children, however, as we have already said, are particularly prone to misconceptions of the world around them; they have less experience to draw upon, and fewer efficient ways of monitoring and testing out what experience they have. An innate fear and credulity may sometimes render them more superstitious than adults, and younger children in particular are very often inclined to take everything at face value; believing, for example, a lot of what they are told by others simply because they hear it said. Parents throughout history have taken advantage of this credulity, often as a way of fobbing off their offspring when it came to answering awkward questions, for example about sex. Indeed this parental willingness to evade and distort the truth is still widely utilized for other purposes, such as forms of disciplinary deception. Threats to leave the child, send him away or call the policeman over some minor domestic naughtiness have all been reported in John and Elizabeth Newson's cross-sectional survey of parental child-rearing techniques in Nottingham.[25] The Newsons sum up this particular parental practice under the heading of 'bamboozlement', and report that it is less effective with children at the age of seven than it was when they were younger. Children have often suffered because of their innate credulity, especially when it was the fashion to terrify them with horror stories over such matters as going to sleep in the dark without daring to make a fuss. Many adult writers, including Dickens, have drawn attention to the mental agony that an older person can cause in a child in this way, whether such stories are told supposedly for the child's own good, or for baser or more thoughtless reasons. In all events, learning to call adults' bluff may be an essential part of the growing-up process; the need for education in the ways of the world, at some level, is a distinctive aspect of childhood in all societies. In this way too, children will always be different from adults, and will always probably be seen as different, however similar some of their needs and the ways they are treated may seem to be.

2/Growth and maturity

Compared with any other animal's offspring, the human baby is born to a state of exceptionally long-lasting dependence upon his mother. He is quite unable to look after himself, and would certainly die without active caregiving. How long this state of dependence lasts is debatable: there have been cases of quite young children fending for themselves, but in general the norm is for a child to be reliant on older people for an extended period, the gradual termination of which often coincides with the end of 'childhood' itself as it is understood in various societies.

A state of initial dependence can perhaps be taken as the first universal feature of childhood. In a sense, man is born very much unfinished; it has been argued that because pelvic size has been limited in human evolution, much brain development has to be deferred until after birth (though as it is birth injury still accounts for a distressing amount of brain damage). Man is the only species where cerebral growth and development persist long into maturity (as late as the age of twenty in some cases). The human brain at birth has in fact reached less than one quarter of its eventual size, whereas higher apes are born with three quarters of their total brain volume already developed.

Because of this initial immaturity, babies and children have often been regarded as completely malleable to adult influences, passively awaiting impressions from the surrounding environment from birth onwards. Until recently only a few psychologists took much informed interest in the young baby as compared with the child after the start of formal education.

But there is by now a quite vast collection of psychological research findings on children, accumulated over the last fifty years, and new techniques for assessing and investigating the young, particularly during the first few months of life, have developed rapidly. It is probably true to say that knowledge of the development and potential of the human infant has doubled over the last decade, and continues to grow at a remarkable rate.

Since we shall be referring to a great deal of psychological data in our attempt to establish what a child is, this is perhaps a good moment to look at the strengths and inevitable weaknesses of the discipline. The psychologist is usually working only within his own culture and time. With his nose pressed up hard against the evidence in this way, it is not surprising that broader trends in childhood development may escape his view, even if he could think up the techniques to measure them. As it is, there are several methods of research at his disposal, none of them perfect. For example, he might try a controlled experiment with children, offering them a problem to solve and carefully altering the situation to discover, say, whether children work better when they are hungry or full of food. If he gets a good result, which in these terms means a clear answer one way or the other that can be statistically validated, there are still other important questions that require his attention. How typical were the experimental children of their own age group and locality, let alone of the majority of children in the rest of the world? How artificial was the experimental situation: would children act differently in their own environments? Did the investigator himself introduce any unconscious bias that may have affected the participants? Could there have been other influences affecting the children's behaviour which were unknown and therefore uncontrolled by the investigator?

Despite these questions, the experimental method has a number of distinct advantages, particularly in studying short-term changes in behaviour or skills. For example, any claim the investigator may make when writing up his results can be checked by replicating his experiment with another sample of children. On the other hand, the experimental approach is less suitable for the study of long-term development, and here psychologists have sometimes preferred simply to observe children over a period in their own natural environment and to report on what they see. This, of course, is the oldest type of psychological inquiry in existence, and much has been learned this way: Piaget laid the foundation for his developmental theory from initial observations of his own children. But not every psychologist is a Piaget, and merely observing and questioning children can lead to very limited conclusions. It is another method extremely susceptible to the observer's own personal bias; his presence, too, may also have a distorting effect upon the behaviour of the child he is watching. As in all psychological investigation, one must ask whether the children observed are a truly representative sample. The psychologist also has the problem of selecting and describing what he actually sees. To record continuously every single aspect of a young child's behaviour over a long period would be impossible; a psychologist therefore must decide what in particular he wants to watch out for. But can he always be sure he is interpreting a child's reactions correctly, especially with the very young who may express themselves inadequately in words? How can he know that he has not missed something vital to understanding a situation? As a mere onlooker, the psychologist has no way of altering aspects of the child's environment to check what the child responds to; he will frequently have to guess why a child does something at any one time. If he wants to avoid this type of psychological speculation, he takes the risk of producing a series of disconnected observations.

Nevertheless, accurate, intelligent observation of children is still the basis for a great deal that is known about them, and is particularly valuable if it produces ideas that can later be tested in more controlled situations. Another useful technique is the 'longitudinal study', where a representative sample of children is followed up over a prolonged period of time. This method allows the psychologist to check differences and similarities between one child and another as they become evident at a particular developmental or social stage. This method has the great advantage that it involves working with extended time spans: there is less risk of becoming diverted by incidental behaviour that may be of little significance in the long run.

Perhaps the first, and certainly the most grisly, longitudinal study I know of occurred some 700 years ago. In a thirteenth-century chronicle, Salimbene de Adam describes how Emperor Frederick II wished to discover what language children would speak if they had spoken to no one beforehand. Would it be Hebrew, the oldest language? Greek, Latin, Arabic? Or the language of their parents? Accordingly, a group of babies was assembled and their wet nurses instructed to care for them physically but otherwise ignore them. In Salimbene's words, because the children 'could not live without the petting and the joyful faces and loving words of their foster mothers' or without the bedtime songs without which a baby 'sleeps badly and has no rest', they all died, and the Emperor's curiosity was presumably left unsatisfied.[1]

It is a pity that the lessons learned here about child neglect were not better appreciated in centuries to come. Later experiments have been more humane, although every now and again one comes across even quite recent studies that seem to share some of the spirit of Emperor Frederick.

Another psychological approach to the study of how children develop is the case-history – a type of psychological biography. If a number of children grow up with distinctive behaviour traits that set them apart from others, it can be instructive to go into their past histories in search of possible causes. In this way, to take one example, early deprivation may be linked with later difficulties in education and socialization.

As always, there are snags. Searching for evidence from the past makes one dependent on other people's memories, and parents can be unreliable in their recollection of their own children. Says Kurt Danziger:

Unfortunately, the considerable investment of time and money in interviewing mothers that characterized the socialization research of the forties and fifties has established little beyond the almost total unreliability of maternal reports. When the mother's answers to questions about her child were compared with independent observations and factual records an embarrassing gap invariably appeared . . . What is more surprising and disturbing is that the mothers proved to be such poor informants even about relatively objective and factual matters like the child's health.[2]

Also, the psychologist must be very careful that he has spotted real causes. Only an adequate control sample (a group of randomly chosen children studied at the same time) will tell him whether other children, faced with the same conditions, have developed in a similar way. It is not enough, say, to suggest a necessary connection between maternal separation and later unhappiness if some children experience the same type of separation in childhood but appear to grow up in a reasonably healthy way.

Even if certain conditions are reliably found to have particular effects, individual children nearly always vary enough in their reactions to pose further questions for the researcher. Can one environment ever quite fairly be compared to another, given that there may still be so many small but important differences between the two situations? Moreover, there is always that most difficult question in developmental psychology – the importance of the individual's own personality (including his genetic inheritance and predisposition) as opposed to the effects his particular environment may have had upon him. Even if we acknowledge the interaction of both factors, this still leaves the respective weightings of personality and environment as a matter for continual dispute. Nevertheless, psychology is still far and away the best tool we have for understanding children, and much of the evidence I shall be using will be drawn from psychological research.

IS THERE AN INBORN SCHEDULE OF DEVELOPMENT?

Psychological studies of recent years have shown that the normal human baby has a number of innate skills and reflexes, which – other things being equal – develop according to a predictable timetable. Some of these skills have been wrongly attributed to the efforts made by those looking after the baby. For example, at a certain stage all children babble; this is not merely imitation of sounds heard, but a spontaneous creation; even deaf infants do it. In the same way, babies smile after the first few weeks, whether they are being smiled at or not; even blind babies – who could not possibly be imitating others – will do this. Many other skills, from grabbing at a moving object to crawling, seem to be part of every normal baby's repertoire. Even the skill of walking, though parents see themselves as encouraging and guiding the first footsteps, seems to owe more to the maturing of nerves and muscles than to practice. An American psychologist, Wayne Dennis, made observations of a pair of twin girls, kept for their first nine months in a state of semi-deprivation, not seeing each other, not spoken to, and taken out of their cots as rarely as possible.[3]* At the termination of this strange regime, however, the children were found to have progressed in many respects at a quite normal rate. One twin found some difficulty in the more complex physical skills, but the other showed no retardation when it came to crawling, walking when led, standing, and eventually walking on her own. Other studies have made the same point: children in most situations will walk when they are ready to.

But it would be oversimple to regard the human infant as merely following a fixed developmental schedule, which always manifests itself at the proper time and place. For one thing,

* One perhaps learns as much about adults as about children from this sort of experiment. It would be easy to write another book on all the bizarre things psychologists have done to hapless children over the years, sometimes even including their own offspring.

there are striking geographical variations: Ugandan children, for example, walk earlier than European children; and among these, Belgian and Swedish infants start walking about one month before French, Swiss and British children. No one as yet has convincingly explained why this should be so, though differences in inheritance, feeding or even physical handling are all possible causes.

Secondly, we must obviously define much more closely what is meant by a 'normal' child in a 'normal' situation. By a 'normal' child we mean one who is neither mentally nor physically damaged, and who has received the basic attention and nourishment necessary for survival and balanced growth. Undernourished children, born to mothers who themselves may have been half-starved during pregnancy, often show a different, retarded developmental pattern. The human foetus will normally form myelin – essential protection for nerve fibres in the brain – towards the end of the pregnancy. A mother who lacks sufficient nourishing food may produce a baby whose 'myelinization' is seriously impaired, and whose mental development is likely to be slow later on. There is argument over whether this type of handicap is reversible, if later efforts are made to help such children (should such efforts be forthcoming). But the initial, retarding effect of under-nourishment cannot be denied.

Even a normal, well-nourished child cannot simply be left to develop on his own, particularly when it comes to more complex skills and learning. However cultures differ in their methods of rearing children, it seems that a certain amount and quality of stimulation and attention directed at the very young is normally necessary, and is provided in response to the baby's own expressed needs. Babies – wherever they are – appear to be born with certain techniques for encouraging this type of attention: smiling, reaching out, ceasing to cry when picked up, and seeking eye to eye contact (even blind babies stare up at their mothers when aware of their presence). These can all be effective in bringing about the kind of interaction and stimulation the baby requires. When in very deprived surroundings this is not forthcoming, the baby's development of basic skills will usually be retarded. For example, whereas an average American child can walk without falling by eighteen months, Dennis in some later work found that very deprived children in an Iranian orphanage were beginning to walk only by forty-five months and sometimes even later.[4] Moreover, Dennis also claimed that a prolonged lack of learning opportunity eventually changed not just the timing but the forms that physical maturity normally take in the young. Thus the Iranian orphans, used only to lying on their backs and then later to sitting up, didn't go on to crawl or walk but instead developed a way of moving about by propelling themselves on their bottoms. This development from their habitual sitting position seems to have resulted from want of any practice or experience in standing up, which they did only very much later.

Such findings qualify Dennis's earlier conclusions; in situations of prolonged deprivation, physical skills like walking may indeed not appear at the standard times. Even more confusingly, it has been suggested recently that some adverse, or even neglectful, social circumstances can actually have the opposite effect – of speeding up motor development in deprived infants.[5] This could be due to an absence of the physical constraints (such as playpens or special baby chairs) by which babies are normally stopped for their own safety from moving around without supervision.

There is still obviously some uncertainty over the timing of development stages. In general perhaps it could be agreed that whereas all normal children develop certain physical skills at more or less predictable times (given overall variations as yet unexplained), the development of other, more complex processes can only be assured by support, stimulation and the opportunity to practise. Even if a baby babbles at the normal time and later goes on to form simple words, his speech will still probably be somewhat retarded if no one ever bothers to talk back to him. In this sense, the child is both initiator and consumer, relying on others but also upon his own innate potentialities. Thus some children may develop more quickly than others, because of a greater genetic endowment, or because of greater encouragement or opportunities to practise provided by those around them.

INDIVIDUAL DIFFERENCES

In this sense, all babies may differ in what they bring to their environment as well as in what they can take from it. There is now an extensive psychological literature on individual differences between children even at the earliest stages of life. For example, very young babies can vary widely in their levels of activity, attention to different sorts of stimulation, physical reactions to stress, tendency to cry spontaneously, and even in their reactions to cuddling (some babies seeming to need and indeed enjoy this much less than others). Psychologists have sometimes related these individual differences to a wider pattern of sex differences, claiming that boys and girls commonly react in dissimilar ways to certain kinds of stimulation. Physiological sex differences, beyond the obvious reproductive ones, certainly do appear at an early stage. Over behavioural differences there is less agreement, although in terms of speed of early development there can be no dispute that girls regularly outstrip boys. How permanent the more individual differences are, and to what extent they influence later development, is not clear, but their existence is not in question, and obviously to some extent they may alter each child's experience of life.

Claims have also been made that personality and body type are connected. W. H. Sheldon suggested three major subcategories of physique: the 'endomorph', round and soft in body build; the 'mesomorph', thick-set, strong and stocky; and the 'ectomorph', the linear type, with a long and delicate bone structure. Important links were suggested by Sheldon between personality and these different physiques: the endomorph, it is claimed, is friendly and easygoing; the mesomorph often aggressive and not very bright; the ectomorph intellectual and restrained. Research findings in this area too are uncertain, but the evidence does suggest relationships of this sort at a crude level, although how significant they might be has yet to be proved.

Psychologists such as H. J. Eysenck and R. B. Cattell have suggested another type of inherent personality difference: between the extravert – excitable and restless – and the introvert – calm but often moody and inflexible. Most people, of course, have both these traits, but it is suggested that individuals who are born with or develop them in more extreme forms will differ in very marked ways, not least as children. Introvert children, it is suggested, are easier to train and learn more quickly than extraverts, who may for instance take much longer over toilet training and who are generally poor at any task demanding concentration. Once more, although these two personality types will emerge in personality tests, there is still dispute over how far children are born with these characteristics and how far they acquire them later. But perhaps enough has now been said about how much any two children can differ to make the point that, in trying to discover what a child is, we must as well as acknowledging certain predictable developmental patterns also admit the presence of strong individual differences, even from the earliest days. How society views the significance of these individual differences will again vary; for the moment, it is enough merely to emphasize their existence.

HOW ADULTS RESPOND TO CHILDISH FEATURES

If children can be so very different from each other, and if the type of stimulation received at home sometimes extends these differences, are there still, on the physical plane at least, common factors one can find for all children? It has been suggested, for example, that babies possess certain physical characteristics that have special appeal for adults: the combination of large eyes, high protruding forehead in relation to a small face, round cheeks, small mouth and a head that is large in proportion to the body.[6] Animals that share some of these characteristics, such as koala bears or kittens, may also release more tender feelings in humans than, say, young birds or fish, which are built on different principles. Certainly, sentimental cartoon films humanize animal faces to make them conform to this sort of baby look. When, for instance, Bambi or Dumbo appear on the screen they generally evoke a groan of appreciation. Rather in the same way, baby-food advertisers regularly choose chubby, smiling toddlers' faces to promote their wares, even though their product may be aimed at much younger infants who do not yet look like this at all.

But even if today's Western audiences do respond in a certain predictable way to this sort of image, the effect cannot be assumed to be universal. History is full of examples of the most revolting cruelty and neglect towards the very young, not necessarily by savage psychopaths but by whole societies, a number of which seem to have found children far from appealing. 'Childhood,' according to one seventeenth-century witness, the French Cardinal de Berulle, 'is the meanest and most abject state of the human condition.' And there were others who shared this view, both then and later. Whether mothers more particularly have certain set reactions to the infant appearance is again open to argument. But granted that the normal infant has features that seem to be universally appealing, including perhaps the shape of his face, whether or not such things work on adults will depend both on the environment in which the child finds himself, and the child-rearing customs in his society. For example, when Margaret Mead studied parental patterns in the Pacific Islands she found that among the Mundugumor tribe, 'women actively dislike their children . . . Mothers nurse their children standing up, pushing them away as soon as they are the least bit satisfied.' Among the mountain Arapesh tribe, however, also from the South Seas, she discovered children who from birth are warmly cherished by their mothers.[7] Both sets of infants will have been born with similar developmental techniques for engaging the attention of their parents, yet in the face of this particular type of behavioural uniformity (such as smiling, babbling and reaching out towards the mother) different cultural norms in each society dictate a totally dissimilar parental reaction.

Some psychologists, working from the study of animal behaviour, have suggested that human beings share a range of common social behaviour, which sometimes manifests itself quite early in life. Irenäus Eibl-Eibesfeldt, for example, has suggested that there are universal signs of embarrassment, where the head is hidden, sometimes in the hands – behaviour found even in children who have been born blind.[8] Claims have been made, on the basis of photographic evidence from different cultures, for common worldwide signs of anger (such as foot-stamping, fist-clenching and teeth-baring) or of fear, sadness and even flirtation. But given that there may be common manifestations of anger and aggression, it is society's reactions to these that again would determine their importance for any one individual. To take these common signs of aggression, for example, as proof that man is inherently aggressive is to beg questions about the extent and frequency of the aggression and how easily diverted it might be into other forms of behaviour. While certain kinds of visible behaviour may admittedly be common, their ultimate significance has still to be resolved.

CHILDREN'S PHYSICAL CAPABILITIES

Returning to more purely physical development, patterns of growth do tend to be broadly similar for all children. As coarse muscle control becomes finer, a child can make more complex and differentiated movements. At the same time his body becomes steadily stronger as his muscle tissue increases and cartilage is replaced by bone. In some societies these changes are reflected in different types of play activity among the young of different ages; for many children, however, the importance of growth lies in its effect on their capacity as potential wage earners. However hard children have worked in the past, and sometimes still continue to work in less developed societies, there are still certain limitations imposed upon them at different stages by their immature physique. For example, children in general appear to need more sleep than adults; attempts to work them for very long and hard hours, as in the early Industrial Revolution, often required the most appalling brutality to keep them awake towards the end of their stint. Many of their accidents, too, seemed to arise from extreme fatigue and consequent inattention.

Once at work, children could of course excel at tasks suited to nimble fingers and small stature, such as feeding, tending and cleaning the factory machines of the Industrial Revolution. The smaller the child operative, the greater the saving of floor space: so long as a child were still able to slip between them, machines could be built very close together. Elsewhere, children were also needed for jobs which involved crawling along narrow passages, as in coal mining or chimney sweeping, or on board ship where the powder-monkey had to scurry along tiny, enclosed spaces. At home, in cottage industries, tasks involving fine manual dexterity were also sometimes better performed by small hands.

Young children, however, could never equal adults when it came to heavier, more muscular work, and to some extent this fact dictated the type of occupation commonly found among working children. For the Royal Commission appointed to look into child labour in 1833, it was at thirteen that 'the period of childhood, properly so called, ceases.' After that, 'the same labour which was fatiguing and exhausting at an earlier period is in general comparatively easy.' On the land, even this might still be considered a tender age for some of the really heavy work. An elderly farm worker, recently interviewed, can well remember the physical strain involved, even for a boy of seventeen or so. 'The difference between a boy and a man at work is that although the boy is strong, he hasn't got the kind of strength to allow him to keep it up all the day. It was this which the men used to mock when I was young. No one liked being young then, as they do now; they wanted to get it over with.'[9] In fact, as long ago as the Magna Carta, the age at which an agricultural tenant was believed capable of husbandry and of 'conducting his rustic employs' was reckoned to be rather lower than this – fifteen. Twenty-one was then the age of majority for everyone 'except the common people, who came of age at 15, and it was only later that 21 filtered down and became the universal age for all classes'.[10]

Children have often begun work as errand boys for these reasons. In farming communities they have commonly been put to jobs such as bird scaring or herding, rather than heavy work like ploughing. For the eleven-year-old Joseph Ashby, for example, working in a Cotswold village in 1870:

> Boys must be there to fetch and carry, flying like the wind for the tools or wedges or nails the men had need of. Looking on, a boy would get absorbed in the men's skill, yet not beyond a certain degree, for it was a boy's deepest disgrace to fail, when a crisis came, to see where his weight was needed to supplement the men's, or when his smaller hand must be thrust in.[11]

This 'looking on', of course, was also a vital factor in eventually learning the job and indeed at this time would be the only work training available.

Thus, although history can provide examples of work where the details of child and adult labour seem very similar, it is important not to overlook the physical differences that will dictate differences in capacity in a number of ways. In this way, glib generalizations about societies where adults and children are supposed to 'share' all the work on an equal basis can be put into a more realistic context.

CHILDHOOD SEXUALITY

Another physical difference between adults and children of course lies in their sexual maturity. At one time, there was thought to be an absolute gap between children and adults: in *Centuries of Childhood*, for example, Ariès quotes long extracts from the diary of Heroard, the physician who attended the Dauphin who was later to be Louis XIII at the beginning of the seventeenth century. Up to the age of seven, the boy was allowed various forms of sexual licence, often freely encouraged in his childish exhibitionism by the adults around him.

Some of this is rather surprising now, even to the most advanced modern taste, but as Ariès explains, 'The child under the age of puberty was believed to be unaware of or indifferent to sex. Thus gestures and allusions had no meaning for him; they became purely gratuitous and lost their sexual significance.'[12] This concept of childish innocence was to last until the end of the nineteenth century, although by that time such frank allusions to sexual matters, at least in the Western world, would have been considered highly improper.

Since the work of Freud, however, children and adults have increasingly been regarded as ranged on a single continuum of sexual interest. Sex play in the young tends to be seen in context, and less often condemned as unnatural precocity. Again, intense pleasure from physical contact, and the strong feelings of love, possession and jealousy are not denied a possible sexual basis, even long before sexual maturity. Yet the difference between a pre-pubertal child and an adult in this respect is obviously quite vast, though it may not be easy to pinpoint. Some anthropologists have reported widespread sexual precocity in the areas they have studied: Ruth Benedict tells us that among most of the Melanesian cultures of South-East New Guinea, for example, children's sexual experimentation is 'encouraged and forms a major activity among small children'.[13] There have also been societies where children are quite unshielded from the sexual activities of adults. Sexual ignorance, as such, can therefore hardly stand as a typical childish characteristic.

The key difference, perhaps, between adults and children lies in children's non-fertility. So long as children have no urgent desires for intercourse as such, and so long as the results of their sexual experiments never lead to pregnancy, then the sexual potential of adults and children will be viewed quite differently. In South-East New Guinea, according to Benedict, 'adults go as far as to laugh off sexual affairs . . . if the children are not mature, saying that since they cannot marry, there can be no harm done'. Thus whether surrounding adults condemn or condone childish sexual behaviour, they will always see it as something essentially different, and as such subject to 'the different mores which almost always govern sex expression in children and in adults in the same culture'. Perception of this difference between adults and children, however variously it may manifest itself in different societies, will almost certainly form a predictable part of any community's attitude towards children, and acceptance of it may be a staple part of all childhood. Many societies institute rites at adolescence, the time of attainment of sexual maturity: a dramatic and clearcut signal of the end of childhood itself.

THE EFFECTS OF SIZE

Finally, perhaps the most basic physical fact about the child is that he is small in a world where those in authority over him will be tall. Whether small stature has any universal implications for all children is hard to say. It means that in terms of height and strength alone, the adult has it in his power to impose his will on children rather than vice versa, and this has almost always been the case. The exaggeratedly progressive, child-centred home or school would appear to be a twentieth-century invention, and even then something more often imagined than real, in the sense that authority is still ultimately vested in the adults. Moreover, children are also potentially at risk among those of their peers who are heavier and stronger than they are, and many accounts of childhood – at least in the Western world – record the experience of being bullied either at home or at school. This physical vulnerability should not be exaggerated, however, for to a large extent it will depend upon the way society organizes itself, and upon its safeguards to protect the young.

What his small size implies in personal terms for the individual child, is harder to say. At an early stage, the infant – unable to distinguish easily between his inner fantasies and external reality – may believe for a time in his own omnipotence. At a later stage, however, he will discover that he cannot order everything as he wishes, and this growing consciousness of his weakness, in comparison with the adults around him, may affect him in various different ways. The realization of physical powerlessness may spur some children to try to master their environment in other ways more suitable for a child, such as through play or through emotional demands on those around them. Other children, perhaps kept very firmly in their place and perpetually reminded of their insignificance, may sink into a more passive role, as if giving up any hope of ever equalling adult strength and competence.

The final outcome for individual personality will obviously depend on the interaction of a number of things: society's general attitude towards the young, parents' specific responses to their children within this framework of opinion, and possibly the strength of the child's own drive towards independence and mastery of his environment. Various schools of psychology tend to emphasize the relative importance of particular factors in this complex equation. In psychoanalytic theory, it is the baby's frustration at his physical powerlessness that is important, and how he deals with these emotions when it comes to comparing himself with, and relating to, the adult parent of the same sex. A social psychologist may look more closely at particular child-rearing modes, and their possible effects upon all infants, while a developmental psychologist may be more interested in what the child himself brings to the situation, in terms of his particular personality structure, and the way in which this interacts with those around him. These are, of course, crudely oversimplified positions, but differences between psychological theories of childhood still make it impossible to agree on the relative importance in early development of such factors as the infant's eventual realization that he is one very small being in a world apparently peopled by giants.

3/The child's personality

A human baby can seem to show very passionate, even violent feeling almost from the first moment of birth. When the baby later feeds on the breast or bottle, he may attack the source of food with something approaching rapacity: for Freud, this was an unmistakable manifestation of sexuality in the young. Before feeding, he may cry in the lusty way that has led many mothers in the past to dope their babies with laudanum or other opiates to stop them waking up the rest of the household. But a crying baby is difficult to suppress indefinitely. St Augustine denounced such early crying as a sin to be eradicated as soon as possible, but even he agreed that the baby might not be able to help it.

However, this is a very partial, Western view of babyhood, based particularly on feeding methods that do not always provide the infant with nourishment on demand. In other cultures, where mothers carry their babies around with them most of the time, and where suckling can take place almost whenever the baby wills it, much less extreme emotion is reported. Crying, which seems to us such a typical part of baby behaviour, may be infrequent, muted and brief.

We are in another area where behavioural characteristics may owe as much to the culture in which they manifest themselves as to any emotion intrinsic to babyhood itself. Within our own culture, there are arguments over the effects of environment even before birth. Does any excess tension a mother may experience during pregnancy necessarily affect the child she is carrying? Is birth itself the trauma that Freud described, leaving us ever after with recurring claustrophobic nightmares of choking in restricted surroundings?

Obviously, a baby will start interacting with his environment immediately he is born, and recent psychological work has drawn close attention to the active ways in which he sets out to master his surroundings. But it is still possible to find some underlying emotions common to all childhood states, even though each culture will always bring out different traits in its children – leading to the sort of divergences that can be so confusing when we are looking for common factors.

ATTACHMENT

At the most fundamental level, a baby must attach itself to older, competent figures in his environment or he will die; he needs a constant food supply and warmth that he cannot provide for himself. We have already briefly discussed in the previous chapter some ways in which infants seek to secure and further this type of potentially life-giving attachment. At what stage the baby's emotions are involved is hard to say, but to the extent that a baby quickly learns to recognize his principal caregivers, he will also appear to show quite soon a kind of pleasure in their presence and, later, grief at their departure. Measuring and labelling such emotions is notoriously subjective; a baby's first smile is very much an instinctive reaction to certain crude stimuli, at least in the early stages. The fact that a baby to begin with smiles impartially either at a mother's face, a hideous mask, or a blank oval piece of cardboard bearing two dark holes as rudimentary 'eyes', suggests that talk of any particularly directed 'love' on the baby's part, at this stage, is hard to sustain. But later, when the child shows a wider range of signs indicating both pleasure and displeasure, it would seem permissible to suggest that he enjoys the presence of certain adults, and enters into simple games of tickling or peek-a-boo with every indication of happiness. Equally, if the baby is thwarted in some way or other, he may then show unmistakable signs of distress.

This dichotomy between pleasure and distress is of course very oversimplified. It has been estimated that there are many different types of crying a baby can produce, and most mothers can quite easily distinguish between, say, an angry cry and a distress cry. The expression of pleasure, too, is similarly complex, and children show an increasing range of emotions as they grow older. For the moment, however, one can say that all normal babies are born with the capacity to attach themselves to other human beings, that they commonly show pleasure in this attachment, and distress when it is interrupted in any vital way.

Such a blanket statement naturally covers a formidable amount of variation, found both in history and in contemporary society. The Victorian literary figure, Augustus Hare, describes a visit in Florence to 'a foundling hospital where all the children were brought up and nursed by goats and where, when the children cried, the goats ran and gave them suck'.[1] This practice could still be found in at least one Italian foundling hospital at the beginning of the twentieth century, and has not been uncommon throughout history. Writing of France in the sixteenth century, Montaigne declared that

> It is common in my neighbourhood to see the women of the village, when they are unable to nurse the children from their own breast, calling in the aid of goats. And I have at this moment two lackeys who never drew woman's milk longer than a week. These goats are very quickly trained to come and feed these little ones, to recognize their voices when they cry and run up to them. If any other but their nurseling is brought to them, they will refuse to feed it; and the child in like manner will refuse to take milk from any other goat.[2]

Presumably, such children might also form strong attachments to their particular animals, although not necessarily: primary attachment is not always exclusively to the provider of food. Rudolph Schaffer mentions an infant sample where 29 per cent 'directed their first specific attachment at several individuals'.[3] Some societies are organized on multi-mothering systems, and babies there might be less likely to become attached to just one person. Margaret Mead, for example, draws attention to societies where a baby might be brought up by anything up to forty different people.[4] Yet even here, at around nine months a baby will still go through a stage where he rejects all but a small number of those who have taken part in his care and upbringing.

Even so, such children may still have less fear of people outside the family than children in a society that favours intensive mothering by only one person. In such societies, a failure by the baby to form this primary attachment, because his principal caregivers cannot give him the attention and stimulation he needs, may be a far more serious matter. Whether or not the effects of this early failure are reversible in later life is a controversial topic in contemporary psychology. John Bowlby, for example, has argued that an early breakdown in attachment may permanently affect an individual's later ability to relate emotionally to others.[5] Other psychologists have disagreed, stressing the inherent adaptability of young human beings. Given a chance to repair early failures through, say, sympathetic fostering arrangements or adoption, they would hold that there is no reason why a once deprived child should not be as normal in his future emotional relationships as anyone else.

This argument is important: are infancy and childhood critical periods, in the sense that certain types of deprivation at this time may have irreversible effects upon the individual for ever after? Childhood has often been thought of in terms of critical periods, for example by Puritans worried about the effects of debased literature on the young, or by nineteenth-century philanthropists like Lord Shaftesbury, convinced that there was no future for children allowed to grow up in an atmosphere of crime.

Certainly, so far as some physical factors are concerned, there are critical periods in infancy and before. If a pregnant mother contracts rubella (German measles) during the first seven weeks of pregnancy, she is very likely to bear a handicapped baby. If a baby is undernourished over a long period, some of his brain functions may not develop normally – and may suffer irreversible impairment. As far as a critical period for the establishment of emotional bonds towards others is concerned, however, the case seems still to be not proven. Sadly, most children who have had a bad start in life are likely to experience further deprivation as they grow older, simply because they will tend to stay in the underprivileged section of society where they began. In this way, they may well continue to receive less attention and care than they need, in the presence of frequently quite inadequate adult models on whom to base their own future behaviour. In this way, the influence of their poor start to life can be formative, as their maladaptive patterns of behaviour are never likely to be modified. Yet given sound and long-lasting remedial help, such children – it is argued – could still recover.

Perhaps the basic point one can salvage from the confusion surrounding this topic is that all children seem equipped to attach themselves to someone, or to several people, in their environment. If they are unsuccessful in their primary attachment, this can have serious effects later on, but there is some argument about just why this should be so. It has been suggested that societies which rely upon institutional or multi-mothering systems for raising children can provide infants with all the care and stimulation they require without any child needing to attach himself primarily to one person. Others would insist that all human beings are born with a capacity to love unique figures in their environment and a need to be loved in turn – and that these emotions must be fulfilled. There, for the moment, we must leave this discussion, with its consequences for our question, 'what is a child?' only partially resolved.

SECURITY, INDEPENDENCE AND FEAR

All babies seem to develop a fear of strangers which tends to become evident during the second half of their first year and is probably linked with their growing ability to recognize more familiar figures in the environment. After the onset of this type of fear, a child will commonly seek refuge with a familiar person when any stranger comes. He will react similarly towards unfamiliar objects and situations. But from a position of safety, perhaps the lap of someone he knows very well, a child may soon feel able to explore new situations, so long as he can always retreat quickly to base in the event of further alarms. Children without the security of a familiar figure at hand may act far less confidently in novel situations. The same tendency can also be found in the behaviour of young apes and other higher mammals at an early stage of development. In some of Harlow's early experiments, whereby baby monkeys were reared in the company of dummy mothers, the infants would still rush to their strange parent and cling to it when something frightening was introduced into the cage, such as a mechanical teddy bear which moved forward beating a drum. After a brief period of clinging, however, an infant monkey would pluck up enough courage to look at the previously terrifying toy bear 'without general alarm. Indeed, the infant would sometimes even leave the protection of the mother and approach the object that a few moments before had reduced it to abject terror.'[6]

Fear is, of course, a basic emotion in all humans: through his genes the child inherits the physical manifestations of fear. One of a baby's earliest instinctive reactions is the 'startle' response, when he first throws out and then bends both his arms and legs at any sudden movement, loud noise or unexpected loss of support. While this particular reaction soon disappears, babies commonly show fear of heights from an early age, and this too is an inborn response, occurring both in humans and in other young mammals long before there has been any genuine opportunity to learn about such dangers.

In later years, some of the fears children experience arise more from their imaginations. Fear of the dark, for example, appears to be an almost universal phenomenon, and children often report fear of the supernatural, even though they may never have had any experiences to account for it. Frequently, frightening stories told to children have been blamed – again no new situation. Children 'begin very early to be susceptible of fear, much sooner than persons not accustomed to them would imagine', warned Dr George Armstrong in 1771, and another medical colleague from the same era, Dr Watson, observed that 'it is still more dangerous to frighten them suddenly with harsh words, disguised persons, stories of ghosts and goblins'.[7]

Charles Lamb described one father, the early-nineteenth-century poet Leigh Hunt, who having himself been harried and sometimes terrified by his brother as a child, was determined to bring up his own son – Thornton Hunt – with 'the most scrupulous exclusion of every taint of superstition'. He 'was never allowed to hear of goblin or apparition, or scarcely to be told of bad men, or to read or hear of any distressing story'. Yet even so, this 'nurse-child of optimism' seemed to have just as many fears as any other child, once put to bed in the dark – starting at 'shapes, unborrowed of tradition, in sweats to which the reveries of the cell-damned murderer are tranquillity'.[8]

Lamb's account here would be of interest to most psychoanalysts, who – in the words of one of them, Dr Ernest Jones – tend to believe that 'young children *spontaneously* create in their imagination, both consciously and still more unconsciously, the same images of horror and terror, and that they suffer from nightmares without ever having listened to a fairy story'.[9] Without going quite as far as this, we could agree that all children are predisposed to experience fear, both real and imaginary, and when questioned young children, at least in the Western world, still commonly talk of supernatural or other fantasy sources of danger rather than more realistic ones, such as fire or road accidents. The search for the young Siegfried – the boy who knows no fear – belongs to myth, not reality. There may be very large individual differences in this area, possibly even at a hormonal level, with some children more disposed to take immediate flight from fearful situations than others. Environmental influences, such as the overstimulation of fear in the young by horrific stories or hell-fire sermons, or the deliberate creation, by conditioning, of fear of certain objects or situations, may also play their part in exacerbating a universal predisposition.

PLAY, AND ITS ROLE IN EXPLORING THE WORLD

As we know, babies are more ready to explore novel objects and situations from a position of security. In fact, this type of exploratory behaviour seems to be common to all children, and is one aspect of the play of all young mammals. Defining play in exact terms is not easy, especially with the very young, so much of whose activity is difficult to characterize with certainty. From the very beginning, all normal thriving human infants seem to want to explore their environments, starting with their own bodies and going on to simple objects around them. Jean Piaget, the psychologist who has done most to bring this early period of development into focus, concentrates both on what the infant sets out to do and on how he achieves his goals. At the first stage of development (roughly the first two years), which Piaget describes as the 'sensori-motor' stage, an infant will clutch at objects, suck them if possible, and turn them round in his hands, inspecting them. He will also take an interest in any simple changes in his environment. A new kind of rattle may attract his attention more than a toy he is already familiar with.

For Piaget, this type of activity suggests that a baby enters the world ready to act upon and to some extent to put into order the different sensations, shapes, sounds and smells that make up his environment. This view was an important development in the psychological concept of the child, and Piaget's research helped discredit the idea that an infant was a largely passive organism, reacting unselectively to any stimulation that happened to impinge upon him. Piaget saw the child as active almost from the start, selecting stimuli from his environment, and welding some of his perceptions into patterned sequences of behaviour or 'schemas' which he could then use to predict or pattern the events around him. In this way, a child will eventually make many discoveries for himself – for example, that an object will disappear if he throws it out of the cot, but (as he also learns later) that such things do not necessarily cease to exist simply because they can no longer be seen.

Not every psychologist subscribes to Piaget's theories, but most would agree that a baby participates more actively in his adaptation to the environment and initiates events more often than was once thought. Play seems a vital factor in this early adaptation, and as such is a universal phenomenon in all normal childhoods. We have already mentioned that emotionally deprived children often do not show the normal child's active curiosity, and there are other abnormal circumstances that may affect children's play. Writing about life in Victorian cities, for example, Paul Thompson mentioned the persistence of play in the young of all classes, save in extreme cases of poverty, where the immediate problem of finding enough food seemed to drive out all playfulness.[10] Much the same sort of thing can still be found in contemporary studies of communities living at this level of poverty.

But play, from an infant's early exploring to the games of older children, seems to be a universal feature of normal childhood. Toys date back to the very earliest civilizations, and throughout history adults have mentioned play as a characteristic of the young, whether human or animal. Evidence for this can be found as far back as the eleventh century, in a contemporary *Life of Anselm, Archbishop of Canterbury*, by Eadmer. St Anselm, 'having begged his parents to send him to school . . . was as a little boy, the story goes, entrusted to a relative who took his duties as a teacher so seriously that . . . he kept the child constantly at his studies and never let him out of the house to play'. Almost driven out of his mind

by this imprisonment, the young Anselm was finally returned to his mother in such a state of anxiety that he turned away from her and refused to speak. In tears at the thought that she had lost her son, his mother decided on a policy of complete permissiveness, ordering all of her servants to let the child do whatever he might wish and not to oppose him in any way; through this treatment he was restored to his former happiness.[11]

This lesson of maternal understanding and insight, however, was lost on many future parents, including John Wesley.
When he founded his own school at Kingswood, he made one
rule 'particularly, that the children should never play'. But
even iron discipline and the added threat 'that a master should
always be present with them' failed to make this rule acceptable or perhaps even viable. In fact, the school itself was
something of a disaster, and even at the time Wesley was
criticized for his ignorance of the 'true nature of childhood'.

The most precocious, adult-oriented children seem to have
played too. The young Macaulay, who according to a maid in
the house talked 'quite printed words' from an early age, was
also said to be 'as playful as a kitten', and used to construct
games on Clapham Common, where a barely perceptible ridge
was always referred to by him as 'The Alps'.[12]

Most psychologists would agree that since many types of
play are found, in some form or other, in so much animal life
as well, it clearly must have a general biological significance. For example, exploratory play would seem to have an
obvious function for any creature that has to adapt itself to
its environment, while individual play with movement, so
often expressed in general intense, physical activity, clearly
has value in developing bodily co-ordination and motor skills.
Some social play, involving games with other children, while
it may have this type of function too, can be important for
other reasons. Imitative games among children, for example,
are an extremely common phenomenon particularly after
infancy, and often reflect behaviour found in the adults of the
species – the little boy playing at soldiers with his friends, or
the girls acting at being mother, for example. But such
examples of sex bias in play immediately raise other questions.
Do boys play aggressive games, and girls play games involving
nurturant behaviour, because it is in their nature to do so, or
because they are simply imitating the adult roles they see
around them? There is no certain answer to this question at
the moment; what does remain true, however, is that this type
of group social play tends to decline sharply around puberty.
Of course adults may continue with forms of play – like certain

sports – which are identical with some of their activities as children. But in other areas there are essential differences between adult and child play, something which has already been argued in a previous chapter.

DO CHILDREN NEED OTHER CHILDREN?

If it is true that social play is commonly found among children, does it follow that all children are naturally social in outlook? To some extent, this question must rest on what we want to mean by 'social'; babies, for example, are social in that they want to attach themselves to other figures in their environment. Will an older child have similar feelings about becoming involved, say, with his peer group?

Let us look at animals again. It is difficult, for example, for a psychologist to teach a very simple learning task to a sheep when it is on its own. Bring another sheep into the laboratory, however, and this most gregarious animal instantly becomes more tractable. No one would argue that human beings are as socially dependent as this, though studies of individuals in prolonged solitary confinement, sometimes self-imposed for the purposes of scientific research, suggest that the condition can be very harmful (although this could be due to a general lack of sensory stimulation). Again, Harry Harlow discovered that a monkey brought up for the first six months with a dummy mother, which could either simply feed it or provide a soft surface for it to cling on to, was strikingly abnormal in its later behaviour as an adult and unable to mate naturally with the opposite sex. When the motherless females of the sample conceived, as a result more or less of rape by experienced males, they mistreated their offspring to the extent that the babies eventually had to be removed for their own safety.[13]

These monkey mothers slightly improved in their second and third pregnancies. But when a similar group of motherless, isolated baby female monkeys were allowed just one hour's play each day with their peer group during their infancy, their later performance as mothers improved a great deal. On the

other hand, baby female monkeys brought up with their
natural mothers, but deprived of all playmates, once again
showed serious deficits in their mothering techniques when
the time came. Thus early experience with the peer group
seems of paramount importance for the later social maturity
of monkeys of either sex.

Is this finding relevant for humans? Certainly, even quite
small babies often react positively to the presence of other
people, old or young – the sound of a human voice alone may
sometimes stop a baby crying. Small babies, from their pram
or cot, will often watch older children playing for long periods
of time, apparently quite absorbed – a phenomenon labelled
'observer play'. Later, a toddler may seem to enjoy the
company of his own age group, even though his rudimentary
language development and general egocentricity make it
difficult for him to play co-óperatively with another child. But
he will happily play his own game alongside other children in
a type of parallel play. Even at this early stage, the child may
quickly learn to discriminate between special favourites and
other children he is less interested in.

As he gets older, and needs less protection and guidance
from home, a child often seems to gravitate even more towards
his peers. There are many practical reasons why this should
be so: societies often band children together by age groups,
for educational or other purposes. The age of a child will
partly determine who is prepared to play with him – it is likely
to be someone at the same stage as himself. A younger child
may have simpler needs and less developed skills; older
children may be out of step in.

There is plenty of evidence to show that children – like
adults – are deeply affected by their experience of their contemporaries, particularly when it comes to imitation, setting
'social norms' such as sex-role identifications, and learning
values, conventions and attitudes. This would seem to indicate that children are at least predisposed towards being
influenced in social matters by a wider group. Parents and
other adults alone will not be able to prepare a child for all the
social forces and tensions that arise from living in a com-

munity of contemporaries. As Bernard Shaw once wrote, 'Old people and young people cannot walk at the same pace without distress and final loss of health to one of the parties.' In a society where children are free to play, at least some of the time, the noise and vigour common to the young would indeed seem to make them natural companions for each other.

There have also always been some solitary children, who seem to get little from their peers and may prefer the company of much older people. Yet how often this represents a free choice, rather than compensation for lack of social skills, or absence of opportunity for socialization with their own age group, is not clear. Such solitary children may still people their games with imaginary friends, and friendlessness at one age may be succeeded by sociability at another. Certainly the norm in many different societies seems to be for first the family and later also the peer group to act as the socializing agencies which shape in the child the behaviour and attitudes acceptable to that particular culture; children who make use of the family only, when other opportunities are there, seem to be exceptional, or reared in rather unusual circumstances.

THE WHOLE PERSON

So far we have considered some common aspects of childhood, such as attachment, fear and play, but in isolation from each other. What of the complete personality, the sum of the interplay of these and all the other emotions that go to make one young human being? Many have tried to find common patterns here, as all the generalizations about 'man' and 'the child' testify. For example, the Christian concept of original sin links all children together in a particular way, giving the teacher or parent the clear task of driving, or sometimes beating, out the bad and replacing it with good – the knowledge of God. Such a message has run through many historical concepts of the child.

In this century early theories of psychoanalysis have sometimes appeared to present another version of original sin in their descriptions of the young. It is impossible to do justice to the complexity of these theories in any necessarily shortened account, but in so far as Freud in particular has had an immense effect upon the twentieth-century image of the child, some attempt at explanation – however inadequate – is still necessary. Briefly, Freud saw babies as the inheritors and in a sense as the direct expression of the instinctual, largely pleasure-seeking energy that runs through all mankind, which he described as the libido. For Freud, a baby is very sensitive to certain areas of his own body: feeding becomes a focus for general erotic feelings, and the baby bitterly resents the onset of weaning, which robs him of the breast – or bottle – which has given him so much oral satisfaction. Later he will become conscious of different sorts of pleasure concentrated in the anal zones. He may violently object to the way his toilet functions, which he is likely to be proud of, evoke general disgust in the adult world and must eventually conform to adult control – the toilet training that can indeed be one of the main areas of dispute between a parent and a young child. In time, the child will have to sublimate whole areas of this early instinctual energy into modes of behaviour that are more acceptable to society. Like adults too, he has to accept a way of life where the instinctive drives which make up what Freud called the 'id' must learn to coexist with those repressive functions existing in each of us as 'conscience' or 'super-ego'. Squashed between the instinctive id and the repressive super-ego is the individual 'ego' that tries to balance these two irreconcilables. The result is a personality – reflected in the society around it – where an essentially fragile stability can only be achieved through a constant process of repression. Later, Freudian theory played down this early instinct theory in favour of a model of man which showed him as more essentially adaptive to the demands of society. Even so, the idea of the personality as something of a battlefield between opposing instinctive and repressive forces was never really lost.

It has been said that neither Freud nor psychology in general ever discovered anything really important about the baby that mothers and nursemaids had not always known for themselves, out of their own experience. However, since his work more attention has been focused, rightly, on the infant's emotions and their strength even at an early age. Partly as a result, mothers are encouraged not to wean their babies too abruptly, but to make it a gradual process. In toilet training, the modern approach again is to be patient with the child, not showing anger or disgust at early failures.

Even so, some of the more specific predictions that Freud made about the later individual development that would arise from unresolved tensions in these areas have not looked very impressive when researched in any organized way. While it may often be true that disturbed children show some of their difficulties in the area of feeding or toilet habits, they do not always carry the marks of this disturbance into later life. For example, Freud suggested that a child who had been toilet trained too early and severely might develop later into what he described as an 'anally fixated' character: in general terms, be overfastidious, obstinate and mean. Again, the child who is weaned prematurely and suddenly may be tomorrow's orally fixated character; a person who always wants more and can never get enough. (These are, in fact, excessively simplified descriptions; psychoanalytic theory would describe character disorders resulting from these fixations in far more detail – although rival schools of psychoanalysis sometimes predict that quite different effects will arise from the same basic trauma.)

In crude terms, both the 'anal' and the 'oral' character types, as outlined above, can be said to exist, but there often seems little obvious relationship between their characteristics and their feeding or toilet habits when children. It seems more likely that infants react to atmospheres as much as to particular practices. Strict toilet training by a mother who is otherwise warm and loving may be a very different experience from the same regime operated by a parent who is cold and rejecting.

Freud's predictions, moreover, are often extremely culture-bound. Attitudes to toilet training are quite different in other parts of the world, where it may be seen as a far less crucial process and be left much more to the individual child to

resolve. The idea that the anal stage inevitably involves con-
flicts for the young is therefore hard to justify, even though
Freud may have often been perceptive about his own society.
The same might be said of weaning: even within our own
time, ways of feeding the young have changed considerably.
In the first edition (1914) of the booklet *Infant Care*, brought
out by the United States Department of Labor's Children's
Bureau, no solid foods at all were recommended until the
baby was at least one year old. Today, the mother might start
on prepared vegetables, fruit or protein for her baby within
the first six months. In this sense, weaning becomes a phased
process from early on, with the baby becoming used to a
mixed diet, combining some solid foods with a regular milk
intake, quite soon. But in a society that relied very heavily on
milk as sustenance for the first two years of a baby's life, a
sudden break to other forms of food might well face the child
with something of a crisis in his habits and expectations. In
modern Western society, however, the changeover in feeding
methods is less dramatic and less noticeable. It is hard to
imagine in these circumstances that weaning still symbolizes
for the baby the withdrawal of love that Freud supposed.

THE OEDIPUS COMPLEX

Perhaps the most famous of Freud's notions on personality
development is contained in his theory of the Oedipus complex, which suggests that every infant boy wishes to possess
his mother and supplant his father (with girls, the theory
works in reverse, where the father is the love object to be won
from the rival mother). When the child eventually realizes
that whatever his efforts (which may include sexual exhibitionism towards his mother and jealous displays directed at
his father) he is never going to succeed, he then retreats into
what Freud called a period of latency. Here the child gives up
his wishes for omnipotence and models himself on his father,
realizing that he will have to develop a genuine masculinity
and maturity before he can achieve his goals.

The theory is open to attack on cross-cultural grounds. The

strict, patriarchal family that Freud experienced in nineteenth-century Vienna, whose life style might often have led to the thwarting of young males, can hardly be taken as a model for societies all over the world, though Freud in claiming that the Oedipus complex was universal appeared to assume that it was. There are, for example, societies where the children do not know their fathers, and examples within our own culture where it is the father who takes on the traditional maternal role.

Before dismissing the notion that the Oedipus complex is an inevitable part of normal development, however, it is worth considering how often jealousy and possessiveness do appear in some form in the lives of children. In literature, too, there are recurrent situations that could be described as Oedipal. Freud, of course, named the complex after the Greek myth, where Oedipus slays his father and makes love to his mother. Folk tales all over the world, sometimes handed on from one culture to another, sometimes springing up independently, record similar stories, where an older, authority figure has to be slain before the hero can win his bride (although such figures are not named as father and mother, they could be said in Freudian terms to symbolize these roles).

Folk tales only survive in an oral culture if people pass them on. It would seem reasonable to suppose, therefore, that those tales that can be found in almost every culture must have some significance for their audience. Looking at the Oedipal myth again, it could be said that it does, in fact, represent in symbolic form the type of development all children must undergo in their progress towards maturity. A child, like the hero, must set out, often with little in his favour and vulnerable to many of the powerful forces around him. He must eventually escape the domination of his elders and attain sexual maturity; could this be one of the processes symbolized in slaying the giant, ogre or dragon and winning the bride? Such stories after all do in a sense describe a universal human pattern. In Ruth Benedict's words,

> The major *discontinuity* in the life cycle is, of course, that the child who is at one point a son must later be a father . . . The

child must be sexless so far as his family is concerned, whereas the father's sexual role is primarily in the family. The individual in one role must revise his behaviour from almost all points of view when he assumes the second role.[14]

In this sense, the Oedipus complex, although possibly not a universal phenomenon, given its exclusively family connotations, reflects a common fantasy of young people faced by a long wait for adulthood and aware of their present immaturity. It is wrong, of course, to imagine that only children enjoy folk tales; even within our own culture, fairy tales were the property of all ages until quite recently. For an older audience, the myth of the hero may hold memories of personal battles won in the past, or relate to recurring fantasies in the mind of mankind. Myth by definition can never be tied down to any particular meaning or need; it always has the capacity to touch on a whole range of experience and imagination.

STRENGTHS AND WEAKNESSES IN THE PSYCHOANALYTIC APPROACH

It would be shortsighted to dismiss all Freud's work simply because it does not follow orthodox scientific lines. Scientific research may only be able to make limited progress in the analysis of a person or of society; some of the most important determinants of personality may always elude psychologists' careful experimental or observational techniques. Freud's views on the emotional turmoil of a child's essential development are sometimes easy to attack, yet they may still make more complete sense of overall human development than the gleanings from academic psychology, which so often tackles only the safer, less controversial sides of human beings, such as their problem-solving ability or perceptual discrimination skills.

Psychoanalysts also have suggested the presence of other universal feelings or fantasies in mankind. Freud believed for example that, while developments such as the Oedipus complex were products of an emotional situation common to all children's lives, we were actually born with what he termed 'phylogenetic' memories. Thus the practice of circumcising the young is based on such an unconscious 'folk' memory, stored away in mankind's brain since the origins of human society, of the elders of the tribe castrating small boys in order to rid themselves of potential rivals. Circumcision since then, therefore, symbolically re-enacts an ancient sacrifice. Carl Jung, Freud's one-time collaborator, took this idea further with his theory of archetypes, which supposed that mankind shared a 'collective unconscious'. This explained for example why certain symbolic forms occur in dreams and art even in very different cultures, and why particular stereotypes are common in world fiction. The universal image of the witch, for example, could be mankind's personification of the child's resentment and suspicion of his mother when she thwarts him in some way, a type of anger strongly emphasized in the writings of Melanie Klein.

The psychoanalytic stress on myth and folk memory, however, is open to the charge that it overemphasizes the inborn side of man at the expense of proper consideration of the social forces that support and mould him into what he is. Instinctual forces, after all, may be adaptable – one culture's view of sex, for example, may be very different from another's. Purely social pressures may in some cases influence the individual's life style, and his satisfaction with it, much more forcefully.

Another psychoanalyst, Erik Erikson, has tried in particular to link psychoanalytic theory with the recognition that social life too is a natural expression of human aspiration, rather than the inevitably repressive force upon the individual that Freud envisaged. Erikson takes some of Freud's basic ideas, but expands them into an eight-stage developmental plan which takes the individual from infancy to old age. The termination of each developmental stage offers something of a crisis to the individual: if he manages it more or less successfully, this will secure him a good base for future growth. If he fails, his development as a person may be seriously endangered.

For example, an infant at the first stage has to develop a basic trust in himself and his environment. For Erikson, this will largely depend upon the feeding experience: is this predictable and pleasurable for the infant, or something hurried and unsatisfying? In general, do the parents support the child when he is frightened or in pain, and is he encouraged in his early skills? If he is enabled in this way to learn to trust his parents and through them the whole adult world, this – for Erikson – enables him to complete successfully his first stage of psychological growth. He is then in a good position to pass on to stage two, brought about by his growing ability to walk and talk. This stage is termed by Erikson 'Autonomy versus shame and doubt' and in a sense corresponds to Freud's anal period, just as the first stage is similar in many ways to Freud's oral stage. The main difference between the theories is that Erikson emphasizes the child-rearing practices that mould such biological dispositions into general kinds of *social* behaviour. The infant, in this sense, is faced by a social as much as an instinctual crisis at each stage. Both Freud and Erikson, though, believe that failure will affect future successful personality development. At stage two, for example, the child begins to work at ways of becoming independent from his parents: new skills of movement enable him to explore the world around him, and growing mental processes help him to make more of his own choices. If things go well, he should start experiencing the autonomy of someone who is largely in control of his own body, including his toilet functions. But if those around him try to press him too hard, and he is made to feel inadequate and ashamed in toilet functions as well as in other ways, then he may not enter the third stage at around four or five – where he should develop genuine initiative of mind and body – with any real confidence or hope of success.

Erikson's theories are well known and influential. They offer a total developmental plan for human beings – still a fairly rare achievement in a subject as fragmented as human psychology. There are critics, however, who from the start have insisted that Erikson's theories are still too narrowly based upon psychoanalytic dogma. For example, is it really necessary to give so much emphasis to oral and anal functions when the baby is soon so busy with other skills and interests?

Could such an emphasis be even less relevant in cultures or periods with fewer preoccupations about hygiene than our own? A modern historian, for example, found when reading through the diary of a seventeenth-century clergyman who, as far as the growth of his children was concerned,

> never mentions anything connected with the natural functions: the attitudes to urination and defecation as well as the location and condition of toilets are never discussed. It is therefore impossible to deduce anything about sanitation and difficult to make an analysis of 'personality types' along Freudian lines. We do not know whether omission reveals disgust, shame or mere indifference.[15]

Many contemporary psychologists would pick out other quite different features of early development as crucial. The American psychologist R. W. White, for example, suggests, rather like Piaget, that the growing child's constant physical activity is witness to his innate need to establish competence over his environment.[16] For White, a child's feelings of inferiority to an adult do not go back to his acknowledgement of genital inferiority at the end of the Oedipal stage, as Freud would have predicted. Rather, they represent the child's wider understanding of his lack of competence in a whole range of skills. He will set about trying to establish his mastery of things, using his parents both as models and as occasional helpers. No other psychological theory, according to White, can possibly account for the sheer energy and constant activity of the young, so often busy without any obvious reward save the pleasure intrinsic to activity itself.

Bertrand Russell once wrote that animals investigated by American psychologists tended to learn tasks by an energetic process of trial and error. The same species, when studied by German psychologists, apparently preferred to sit down and wait for a flash of insight. Is the behaviour White describes universal, or is it the product of a vigorous, pioneer society, where 'getting on', whether by babies, businessmen or psychologists, has a significance not always found in other cultures? Again, what role do individual differences and

genetic inheritance play? How do they interact with the style
of upbringing and the specific adult models of behaviour with
which the child may be expected to identify?

This chapter will have made clear some of the difficulties
that arise when one attempts to suggest any universal models
for behaviour and for the emotions, of which only a few have
been examined in this chapter. Are other emotions, such as
sympathy, shame, envy, pity, awe, also common to all human
beings, and therefore found in all children at some stage?
There have been endless arguments over this sort of question,
but over and above a limited number of basic drives, universal
patterns of emotion and motivation become hard to demonstrate. This does not, of course, necessarily imply that they do
not exist. All the theorists so far discussed may seem to be
right about some children some of the time; perhaps for the
moment this is as much as we can hope for from a science, like
psychology, that is relatively new. Whether we can be more
certain about universal patterns of intellectual growth is
something that will be explored in the following chapter.

4/The child's mind

ORGANIZING SENSATION

'The baby,' according to William James, 'assailed by eyes, ears, nose, skin, and entrails at once, feels it all as one great blooming, buzzing confusion' (often misquoted – with 'booming' forming a tempting substitute for 'blooming').[1] But is James right? Modern research techniques suggest that from the first moments babies are capable of discriminating between many of the sights and sounds that surround them. Confusion and stress generally arise only when a baby is presented with stimulation that he finds overwhelming, such as very loud noises, or a profusion of bright, complex shapes too close to his eyes. Otherwise, far from being 'assailed' by all the sensations coming to him, a normal baby seems to welcome a stimulating environment, and almost immediately sets about organizing it into manageable proportions.

Much of our understanding of how he does this is due to Jean Piaget. It is hard to overemphasize the importance of his contribution to the concept of the child that has developed in this century. It would be fair to say that before Piaget no one was particularly interested in the intellectual growth of babies as something important in its own right and with its own rules and mannerisms. Instead, psychologists tended to see infants' developing intellects primarily in terms of how closely their type of thinking approximated to adult thought. Thus a normal baby was thought gradually to pick up those adult mannerisms and speech habits common in his environment. His thinking would then come to resemble an adult's, though lacking the knowledge that education would in time supply. An intelligent child was therefore one who was forward in, say, historical or scientific knowledge, and biographies of eminent men often stressed this type of precocity.

There is much that is true in this picture; intelligent children may have unusually retentive memories for some of the details of adult knowledge around them. But Piaget's principal contribution, perhaps, has been to show that in many ways young children, whether noticeably bright or not, do not reason in the same way as adults. On the surface there may be similarities, but once children's thinking over a whole range of problems and topics is analysed (in the way Piaget did with his own and other children) typical structures tend to emerge. These, in turn, seem to follow certain developmental patterns. Studies of children in other cultures seem to support the view that children think in a way that is intrinsically different from adults – something that is of great importance in our search for common factors in childhood. But do all children think in the same way at similar periods of their lives?

INTELLECTUAL DEVELOPMENT ACCORDING TO PIAGET

Before attempting to answer such a question, it would be as well to sketch in some of the developmental patterns that Piaget outlines, and the reasons for the shape they take. As we have seen, Piaget always stresses that a child initiates his own learning, and that he is born with the desire to assimilate his discoveries about the world around him into mental patterns that will enable him to make simple suppositions and predictions about it. Returning to William James again: it is true that the newborn is presented with literally millions of different stimuli which are constantly developing and changing. Piaget suggests that, faced by this state of flux, the baby is naturally geared to make as much sense of it as he can, picking out simple patterns in time and space, and learning to adapt his behaviour accordingly. For example, he may learn that the sound of his mother's step by the door, in conjunction with a sensation of hunger in his stomach, is likely to result in feeding. This in turn may lead him to make anticipatory sucking motions. At other times, he may put other items of early experience to the test: he may explore further a favourite toy, or some particular cause and effect he has stumbled upon – for instance, pulling a cord that makes a mobile above his head move. This sort of activity, it is true, is not very different from the learning by association that was such a popular idea with nineteenth-century British philosophers like Herbert Spencer or John Stuart Mill. But Piaget constantly stresses the almost ceaseless activity of babies; far from lying inertly waiting for something to happen that they can then interpret, they seem to seek out, practise and perfect early skills for their own sake. For example, a baby's babbling, once thought of as a pleasant but mindless pastime, is now seen – among other things – as a way for the baby to practise the sounds he has picked out from adult speech.

This type of practice, according to Piaget, is of central importance: the baby is constantly modifying the patterns he has established from experience by adding new information and perceptions which he gets from his exploratory activity. Piaget describes this process as accommodation. It should be clear that from the beginning a baby's growing understanding will be based both on the observed consequences of his actions and the modifications to his mental structures brought about by his increasing knowledge of the physical world. Much later, when he is old enough to be told things by others, most of what he hears this way will make sense and become genuinely integrated into his personal mental schema only if it relates to his previous stock of experience. Thus a child cannot be seen merely as a miniature adult, passively soaking up other people's knowledge. Rather, he will absorb experience only in so far as it seems relevant and can be understood; not surprisingly, some of the knowledge he absorbs in this way may emerge as rather different in shape and content from when it left his parent's or teacher's lips.

For example, anyone trying to explain the mysteries of sexual reproduction to a five-year-old in too much clinical detail should not be surprised if the child restructures the information to fit his own immature understanding. A child at an early age will not react in a detached, scientific way to any discussion of physiology; he is bound to try to integrate new facts into the more simple scheme of things he already has. An example from Kornei Chukovsky makes this point:

Five-year-old Volik Schmidt reacted in this manner when his mother openly discussed with him, at length and in detail, the process of procreating babies. He began at once to improvise a long 'novel' about his life in his mother's womb:
'There was a partition there . . . between her back and her tummy.'
'What kind of partition?'
'The kind with a door. The door was very tiny. Yes, yes – I saw it myself when I was in your insides. And there is also a tiny, tiny room there. A little uncle lived in it when I was in your tummy . . . I visited him, drank tea with him. Then I played in the small garden. There was a little garden there too – with sand in it. And a little wagon . . . I played with the kids there and took rides with them in the little wagon.'
'How did the kids get there?'
'They were born to the little uncle. Many, many children. And all of them were boys – there were no girls.'
'And you lived with them?'
'I often visited the little uncle, and when it was time to be born I said good-bye, shook hands with him, and came out of your belly.'[2]

It is easy to see that young Volik can only visualize his mother's womb in terms of the domestic architecture and general experience already familiar to him. Piaget described such early thought processes as 'egocentric', not implying selfishness but rather the way in which the young inevitably see the world from their own very subjective point of view. Personal experience is, after all, the only thing a child can draw upon; it has made sense up to now and there is no reason to change it – until future events suggest modifications which bring it closer to an adult reality. Thus it may be natural for a small child to think that it is his going to bed at night that causes the sun to go down, rather than vice versa; the two events usually go together, and the child may be used to ordering other events in his life, demanding food or attention from others as the mood takes him.

ANIMISM

In Piaget's words, 'So long as the child supposes that everyone necessarily thinks like himself, he will not spontaneously seek to convince others, nor to accept common truths, nor, above all, to prove or test his opinions.' One example of this, perhaps, can be found in the phenomenon of animism, which involves the attribution of human thoughts and emotions to non-human organisms, a process which Piaget describes as a stage of every normal child's intellectual growth. Thus, doors may be punished for swinging on to small hands, toys praised or blamed, and the family car given a Christmas present. The whole process, and some of the ways in which it gradually comes to be replaced, has been described by Nathan Isaacs, one of the first psychologists to popularize Piaget's ideas in the English-speaking world.

> The child doesn't *believe*, for example, that 'everything is alive'; he simply doesn't *know* that 'everything isn't alive'. He simply turns to all kinds of things with the expectations, or the habitual modes of behaviour, which he has in fact drawn from his experience of living things. He does not *know* that locomotives don't want biscuits – how should he? He doesn't know this until he offers a biscuit to a locomotive (or things like it) and the locomotive takes no notice whatever, behaving quite differently from his brother or the dog.[3]

Since his early work on children's broader ideas about themselves and the world around them, Piaget has preferred to investigate more specific areas of children's thinking. His more recent work, for example, has tended to centre on certain problems to do with children's perception. While he has himself sometimes questioned the efficiency of some of the research techniques used with children in his early work, his general findings from this period of his research have nevertheless stood the test of time extremely well, providing researchers since then with useful hypotheses to test for themselves. A number of psychologists, for example, have tried to discover whether animism is a universal thought process, given that in a Western culture traditional stories and nursery rhymes such as *The dish ran away with the spoon* may actually instil or at least encourage animistic thinking from an early age. Margaret Mead, for example, claimed to find no evidence of animism in her studies of the Manus children of New Guinea. But her conclusions have been challenged by a psychologist, Gustav Jahoda.[4] He points out that the child's belief in animism stems from an early inability to dissociate the inner from the outer world, leading to his 'introjecting' external objects with some of his own thoughts and feelings. Some of this introjection may happen at a time when the child is still at a very simple stage linguistically, so that it is difficult to elicit information about his mental processes through questions. As he grows older, he may discard his animistic ideas as they prove inappropriate to later experience, but only then may he have the linguistic ability to answer researchers' questions on animism. In Jahoda's own study of children in West Africa, he was able to confirm that some of the responses given to him by younger children were clearly animistic. Such responses declined with age, and were not necessarily elicited from all children. Nevertheless, since the younger the child the greater the animism, Jahoda may indeed have found a universal trend which had previously eluded researchers because of linguistic difficulties. Even if young children do show a more adult understanding of the inanimate in some examples, this does not rule out the possibility of animistic thinking in others. We should not expect children to be consistent in their intellectual approach: as Nathan Isaacs pointed out in the passage already quoted, their learning is bound to be patchy, and to depend to some extent on the experiences they have already had.

If early belief in animism is a universal trait, it would follow that other evidence of egocentricity (in Piaget's terms) would also be found in children's early mental processes, whatever the culture, and to a certain extent this appears to be so. Where geography is concerned, for example, a child may begin by imagining that the place where he lives is the centre of the universe; only later may he be able to place it in a wider scheme of things. Gustav Jahoda, again, this time studying children aged from six to eleven in Glasgow, found a natural progression from a child's simply knowing about the immediate street he lived in, to seeing it as part of Glasgow, to seeing Glasgow as part of Scotland, and finally to being able to place Scotland in the context of the United Kingdom. At each of the earlier stages, children were unable to think in terms of a wider context.[5]

There have also been a number of studies made of children's conceptions of time. Small children live very much for the moment, putting everything in the past under one blanket term such as 'yesterday'. Even older children sometimes find it hard to think of the past in terms of any ordered succession of events, so that a grandmother, Guy Fawkes and Julius Caesar may all be imagined as living at the same time. Only later is the past seen in a longer time span than that covered by a few generations. Again, so far as duration of time is concerned, it seems common for children to think first simply in terms of days, and then weeks, before longer spans such as seasons or years are really comprehended – possibly not until the age of seven. Once again, the young child starts out from his own essentially egocentric viewpoint; only later is he able to divorce his concept of time from the immediate here and now.

It would be wrong to suppose that exactly the same sorts of ideas about geography, history or time would necessarily be found in all children. Much will depend upon the local culture which the child is trying to make sense of, so that children in different societies will reflect in their early intellectual development their society's ideas on these topics. Even so, there may still, because of the common egocentricity of children, be similarities in the way they think about the diverse cultures in which they are born. Piaget suggests a number of common, early intellectual patterns. There is finalism, for example: the belief that everything is designed for the express use and convenience of man, so that the sun comes out and then follows us just in order to keep everyone warm. The child will always look for a purpose, since for him everything in nature has some kind of justification and motivation. In turn, this leads to the notion of immanent justice, in which the universe shares man's purposes. In this moral universe, there can be no coincidences or meaninglessness. To use one of the situations Piaget commonly put to children, if a thief stole some money and ran over a bridge which broke under him, the bridge would break – according to the young children who were asked – because it was a *thief* who ran over it, not for instance because the planks were rotten.

It can be seen how closely this type of thinking is linked to the childish animism already discussed. To this, Piaget adds a third thought process, which he terms realism. For Piaget, realism (and as usual his sense has little connection with the standard meaning of the word) describes the way in which thought and action are often confused in a child's mind, so that if he wishes for something to take place he may sometimes see this wish as the equivalent of actually making it happen – a kind of magic, in fact. This lack of differentiation between the self and the outside world (where indeed a child has difficulty in distinguishing between physical and psychological effects) helps explain why younger children commonly believe that their dreams are real experiences. In this way, thoughts, wishes and feelings may get confused with the ability to affect and change things in the physical world, so that a child might ask his parent to stop it raining outside. Later, the child may believe that he can do this himself, if he wills it hard enough. At another level, if a small child has a very strong fantasy about something he would like to have happened, he may end up by quite sincerely believing in its objective truth.

DO CHILDREN AND PRIMITIVE ADULTS THINK ALIKE?

The illusion of omnipotence running through children's thought processes at the egocentric stage brings to mind similar aspects of thought in historical and primitive societies, as well as reminding us of incidents and practices in our long tradition of folk and fairy stories. If such thought processes can be found almost universally, this would seem strongly to support both Piaget's theories and the idea of a common childhood for man, from which each may or may not grow according to the level of education available to him. The idea that primitive, pre-industrial man naturally thought like a child, and that the growth of each individual's mental processes recapitulates the development and history of civilization itself, is now discredited. Modern anthropologists have shown that, while attitudes to nature, totemism and other institutions in the primitive world may indeed display a type of animism also found among children, primitive man's thought and behaviour in other areas of life can be quite as rational as anything found in more advanced societies. Says Raymond Firth: 'In nutrition, technology, economics, law and the activities of family and kinship we have seen the primitive as a reasonable being. His solutions to the vital problems that confront him, though they are often different from ours, appear to us as alternative rather than illogical.'[6]

Again, the supernatural beliefs of primitive man are now more commonly seen as an integral part of the whole practical social world in which he has to live: a mythopoeic back-up, as it were, to the social bonds that hold any society together. To expect a consistently *literal* belief in various rites and rituals would be to repeat the sort of mistakes sometimes made by nineteenth-century anthropologists. Rather, primitive man can on occasion be as objective about the myths that bind his society together as we can be about ours. Mary Douglas quotes the following: 'Once when a band of !Kung Bushmen had performed their rain rituals, a small cloud appeared on the horizon, grew and darkened. Then rain fell. But the anthropologist who asked if the Bushmen reckoned the rite had produced the rain was laughed out of court.'[7] One can imagine the same reaction from representatives of the National Farmers' Union if a rainstorm followed immediately upon the Archbishop of Canterbury's fulfilling their request that he pray for rain. In fact, such requests were often officially made in times of drought at the annual general meeting of the Union, and were until quite recently regularly announced on the news bulletins of the BBC.

So while it is facile to equate the thinking of primitive man with that of a child, Piaget is probably right to insist upon the frequent convergences between adult and infantile thinking, whether among primitive men, pre-Socratic Greeks, or in less guarded moments among adults in our own society. Egocentric thought, as defined by Piaget, does appear to be a forerunner of all later human intellectual development, in whatever society, and its ubiquity suggests that it is indeed a universal stage of mental growth in children and in some cases continues into adult thought processes too. As Piaget puts it himself,

> To sum up, where there is convergence between the thought of the child and historical representations, it is much easier to explain the latter by the general laws of infantile mentality than by reference to a mysterious heredity. However far back we go into history or prehistory, the child has always preceded the adult, and it can be assumed that the more primitive a society, the more lasting the influence of the child's thought on the individual's development, since such a society is not as yet capable of transmitting or forming a scientific culture.[8]

Examples of infantile animism and omnipotence persisting into adult thought are not hard to find. Reports of magic, where thoughts – in the form of spells – are believed to affect those at whom they are directed, are commonly found both in anthropology and history. Similarly, pre-scientific attempts to make sense of and find order in the world have often led to the impersonal universe being invested with human motivations and desires. Thus natural disasters may be attributed to divine anger; and good happenings taken as evidence that the same divine government has been appeased – perhaps by human intervention in the form of sacrifice, ritual or prayer.

There is no need to look only to anthropology for examples of some of these beliefs, when there are so many available from our own past. The French historian Lucien Febvre has stated that the mental equipment of a sixteenth-century Frenchman quite lacked concepts as important to us now as 'causality' or 'regularity', and any sense of the impossible. Everything had to have an explanation, and in the absence of a more detached, scientific insight, people accepted a magico-humanized universe, where dreams might foretell the future, and omens were taken seriously. In this world, animals were sometimes thought to behave like humans, and even inanimate objects, like stones, had the power to take on human shape and movement.[9]

The intellectual climate of sixteenth-century England has recently been described in rather the same way by Keith Thomas.[10] In church, the sacrament was believed to have magical properties for those who took it, and prayers were recited as if they were charms in situations where people wished to ward off evil luck – for instance, when searching for medicinal herbs. A great many things were thought to possess magical properties, including colours, letters and numbers. A parent's blessing or curse was held to be enormously significant. Turning to folk or fairy tales, one again finds talking animals, magic and spells and a moral universe where streams or forests may allow the free passage of the hero but turn back the villain. In stories as in real life, dreams and omens were thought to be accurate prophecies of the future, and lucky charms could make all the difference between success and failure. We can also find evidence of another egocentric thought process described by Piaget, artificialism – the belief that all the objects and events in the world were made by men for men. Thus the shape of a certain mountain, or the position of some standing stones might be explained in terms of the actions of a mythical hero or villain, ever after recorded in folk lore. Similarly, magical, anthropocentric explanations might be offered for everyday phenomena, such as why the sea is salt. Children, sharing as they do some of the same beliefs and conventions, enjoy such stories now; once, however, they were equally important to adults too, and in primitive societies today public storytellers are still popular figures.

Even in the developed world, egocentric beliefs survive in adult thought. There is plenty of evidence that forms of superstition, exemplifying some of these quasi-magical thought structures, are still extremely widespread. In a lecture on modern folk lore, given to the Anthropology section of the British Association, A. M. Shearman – discussing those stories we tell that always happen to 'someone else' – maintained that 'Aspects of magical beliefs, cautionary morals, "divine" or "natural" justice, racial feeling, divine providence (can) be seen in the tales and this element plays a major part in their attractiveness and credibility'.[11] Another anthropologist, Geoffrey Gorer, has made the same point: 'About a quarter of the population . . . holds a view of the universe which can most properly be designated as magical.'[12]

DIFFERENCES BETWEEN CHILDISH AND ADULT THINKING

This infantile element in adult thought should come as no surprise; Piaget himself admits to quite irrational behaviour when his car breaks down, involving 'empirical trial and error at a very low level. At other times I go even lower and almost give way to magical behaviour.' Other experimenters have found quite a large overlap between children's explanations of why something happens and those of some adolescents and adults. The difference, however, between adults and children in this respect is that while adults can develop more stringent forms of logic and abstract thought, children up to a certain age simply do not seem to have that power. In a primitive society there may be less of a gap between the thinking of an adult and that of a child, although to imagine that the animistic ideas of a primitive adult resemble those of his children in every detail is as reasonable as supposing that the religious beliefs of the Pope are identical to those of a Catholic junior school pupil. In some areas an adult may indeed think along broadly similar lines to children, but usually in a great deal more detail and general complexity. He may also retain in many areas of his life a type of wisdom drawn from his greater knowledge of the world he lives in, that is beyond the more limited, inexperienced understanding of most children. Raymond Firth has written:

> In the *Missionary Notices* of 1829 it is recorded that some missionaries talked to some Maori about the resurrection of the dead, when the following remarks were made by natives: 'How many persons have already been raised from the dead? Did you see them?' Being answered in the negative they laughed heartily, saying 'Oh! Indeed! You only *heard* of it from someone else.' When ideas of this order are not backed up by their own traditions and current tales, natives are often ready to adopt this disconcerting commonsense attitude.[13]

And in other areas of skill such as technology, as we have already said, the adult's understanding and control of the task in hand will be way beyond that of the child.

In an educated society, the gap between adult and child thought may be different in kind as well as much greater in detail, and may exist in more areas. Not that the adult will always think in this more complex way; we should never suppose that, as we move from one developmental thought stage to another, we leave every element of the simpler type of thinking behind. In Piaget's view, though, one crucial area where this gap obtains is in the development of concrete and abstract thought; this is important both for his theory and for any understanding of the nature of childhood intellect.

Piaget sees intellectual development as progressing in four successive stages: the sensori-motor period (lasting from birth to two); the pre-operational period (lasting from about three to eight); the period of concrete operations (lasting from about eight to eleven) and the period of formal operations, which usually begins around eleven or twelve and forms the basis for abstract thought. All these stages will be discussed in more detail, but for the moment it might be useful to concentrate on the last two stages, of concrete and formal operational thought.

Very crudely, operational thinking, in Piaget's terminology, describes thought that is logically structured. While a small child thinks intuitively, often being unable to describe quite how he has arrived at his conclusions, a child who has succeeded in operational thinking follows a more logical path, and is able if need be to retrace the steps he took in his argument. The type of intellectual development that makes this possible will be discussed shortly; for the moment, the chief difference between the third stage – concrete operations – and the fourth – formal operations – is the ability to reason abstractly. A child at the stage of concrete operations can think logically about tangible situations or events. He may show this ability in tasks where objects must be placed in sequential order, compared, or seen in other logical relationships with each other. But at the level of *formal* operations a child can reason abstractly without needing to manipulate or think about actual situations or events. This means that he can reason about the hypothetical, and indeed can think about thinking itself, both forming hypotheses and then testing them. The child who can think in this rational and systematic way can obviously detach himself more easily from the here-and-now that dominates the younger egocentric child. Indeed the formal operations stage can be seen as the necessary basis for all genuine intellectual exploration.

Although Piaget states that children begin to enter the stage of formal operations by the age of eleven, this is by no means true of all children everywhere. Cross-cultural psychologists report that this type of formal logic and abstract thinking seems to depend on the presence of advanced forms of education. Without this, a whole society may remain at the stage of concrete operations, a type of thinking which in itself is quite suitable for the needs of an agricultural culture before it has moved into the more complex economy that necessitates a more abstract approach.

This indeed may be one of the most vital differences between a primitive and a developed society, so far as different styles of thought are concerned. Looking for such a distinction, a modern anthropologist, Mary Douglas, makes rather the same point:

> There is only one kind of differentiation in thought that is relevant, and that provides a criterion that we can apply equally to different cultures and to the history of our own scientific ideas. The criterion is based on the Kantian principle that thought can only advance by freeing itself from the shackles of its own subjective conditions. The first Copernican revolution, the discovery that only man's subjective viewpoint made the sun seem to revolve round the earth, is continually renewed. In our own culture mathematics first and later logic, now history, now language and now thought processes themselves and even knowledge of the self and of society, are fields of knowledge progressively freed from the subjective limitations of the mind. To the extent to which sociology, anthropology and psychology are possible in it, our own type of culture needs to be distinguished from others which lack this self-awareness and conscious reaching for objectivity.[14]

To bring the argument back to children: in an educated, industrial society the division between concrete and abstract modes of thought could indeed be taken as one of the absolute differences between the child and the adult. Children cannot reason in a genuinely abstract way until they reach a certain stage, which in itself will depend upon previous education, chronological age and maturation. An older, adolescent child or adult, however, should normally have the ability to think more objectively, given a supportive culture and educational system. Adolescents and adults may not think in this way all the time: sometimes such forms of thought may hardly be used at all. But they should be at an educated adult's disposal when he wants them, in argument or thought that demands a certain degree of abstraction.

If this were the only intellectual division between adults and children, we should have to assume that there were no significant intellectual differences between the generations in less developed societies, where abstract thought – in Piagetian terms – is not found. We have seen that this is a narrow and oversimplified view. In fact, looking both at such societies and at our own history, it is possible to suggest a number of other absolute differences between adult and child thought, again within the Piagetian framework, which manifest themselves at an earlier stage than that of formal operations.

Going through Piaget's developmental stages again, but this time starting at the earliest, the sensori-motor stage, we find there is a quite obvious difference between adult and child ability, which has always been recognized. At this stage, the child does not so much think as act, manifesting his growing intelligence through his actions. He soon learns, for example, that objects have a permanent existence; if his mother hides a toy under a blanket, an older baby will try to find it, whereas a younger child may lose interest, as if it no longer existed when it could not be seen.

The acquisition of this concept of 'object permanence', together with the development of language, comes at the end of the sensori-motor stage and the beginning of the pre-operational period, marked particularly by the type of egocentric thought already discussed. The child may now be thinking about his environment, but unable to see things except from his own essentially limited point of view. At the same time, his thinking will be dominated by simple perception rather than logic, and is described by Piaget as pre-operational precisely because of its intuitive, sometimes irrational quality; a child at this stage is frequently unable to comment upon his way of arriving at an answer, and indeed may not necessarily be able to come to the same conclusion twice over. At this stage, stories and accounts of actions may ramble from an initial situation, the child sometimes forgetting where he started out from, or how he got to his present position.

Perhaps the difference between this mode of thought and the next stage of concrete operations can best be shown by describing one of Piaget's most famous experiments. A child is faced with two identical balls of clay, which he and the experimenter agree are quite equal. The experimenter then rolls one ball into a sausage shape in front of the child, and asks him whether the amounts of clay are still the same. A child at the stage of concrete operations will say that they are; a pre-operational child will commonly insist there is now more clay in the sausage shape, supposedly because it looks longer (if an adult were shown the sausage and the ball, not knowing that they contained the same amount of clay, he would very probably say the same, forced to use only the evidence of his eyes).

Piaget has sometimes been criticized for his use of verbal instruction in these early experiments; could a small child in fact be confusing the idea of 'more than' with the idea of length? Yet when these experiments have been repeated under modified conditions, the answers are still strikingly uniform, even from children of different cultures. Given some local variations, children up to the age of seven or so tend to answer one way; older children and adults will respond in a more logical manner.

For Piaget, what primarily separates the two groups is the notion of conservation – roughly the idea that any substance remains the same in certain properties (provided of course that nothing is actually added or taken away from it) even though its external appearance may have changed. This idea of the essential invariance of matter, beyond superficial changes of appearance, has great significance for Piaget's view of the intellectual development of the individual. The failure of a pre-operational child to understand the experiment with clay, or any of the other experiments to do with the conservation of liquids, number or other properties of objects, implies for Piaget that the child cannot think in terms of two dimensions at once: he can only 'centre' on one at a time. But an older child can see that the length of the sausage of clay and the roundness of the ball of clay compensate for one another. Besides, unlike the pre-operational child, he will be able to structure the present situation in terms of the immediate past; by remembering that the two balls of clay were originally the same, and then picturing the transformation of one ball into a sausage, an older child shows his ability to reverse thought from end-point back to initial situation, which Piaget defined as essential to any mental operation.

The significance of this particular mental step forward should now be becoming clearer. Basically, trying to understand the world from the evidence of simple perceptions alone is unsatisfactory; the eye can be so easily misled. The child needs to grasp some of the properties which do not vary according to appearance. As Jerome Bruner puts it:

> In time, the child recognizes that there is constancy across change in appearance. What he is doing in the process of mastering invariance is, of course, constructing increasingly stable models of the world, increasingly comprehensive ones capable of reducing the surface complexity of the world to the limits of his capacity for dealing with information.[15]

Without this ability, any reliable (if rudimentary) conception of time, space, number, or logic would be beyond the individual. To that extent he will remain a slave to immediate sensation, perpetually at risk from perplexity and contradiction, and without the benefit of logical structures to pattern diversity more predictably and efficiently.

Operational thinking can also help the individual to make better use of previous experience by linking the past meaningfully to the present. He is no longer tied to the immediate here-and-now. The ability to think both forward and in reverse will enable him to form plans and hypotheses (although at this first stage only about concrete objects or situations) and then to test them out in his mind, checking a thought sequence for obvious gaps in logic.

Another feature of Piaget's description of this stage of development is what he calls the phenomenon of 'decentring'. As we have seen, a small child sees everything from his own point of view. For example, in another of Piaget's experiments children were shown a doll sitting on a chair looking at a three-dimensional toy mountain plus accompanying scenery, placed on a table top. The child was then taken round this model and asked, at different angles the guess how the same scene would appear if he were still seeing it from the vantage point of the doll – his answer taking the form of choosing a picture that he imagined would accurately illustrate such a different perspective.

The result was that younger children chose the picture of the scene identical with the one they could see with their own eyes, even though they may have been looking at the scene from an angle of 90 degrees to the doll's hypothetical line of vision. Children of between six or seven, however, sometimes chose a picture that was not the same as the one they could see from their particular vantage point, although it might still not coincide with the picture the doll would see. It was only the children from eight or nine upwards who were nearly always accurate in their choices.[16]

Decentring, then, is the ability to see things from another point of view, in this case quite literally. This other point of view may be distinct from what the child is immediately conscious of, whether in time (remembering the clay sausage when it was once a ball), space (appreciating the necessarily different views of the toy mountain as viewed from different angles) or social understanding (how might another person feel about the same situation?). The emergence of some form of empathy, however rudimentary, is of enormous importance to the developing child, and to the human race as well. No other species has the ability to place itself imaginatively in the position of others. It is, of course, an ability that very often eludes adults as well as children, sometimes to the cost of civilization itself. But some feelings of empathy are essential if the child – or man – is ever going to learn to understand others. Later this understanding of others' feelings may influence the area of moral judgement, so that early absolute judgements on complex issues often come to be superseded, given increased maturity and a society that encourages such discussion, by a position more related to individual circumstances.

As well as beginning to decentre in this way, the operational child now has the ability to think in two dimensions simultaneously, as we have seen. This does not apply only to experiments with clay or water; it affects almost every mental operation. For example, it may be difficult for a pre-operational child to grasp that a *doctor* can also be a *father* at the same time, or that a *father* can be a *son* and a *brother* too, although a child of eight or so can understand this perfectly well. Such a tendency to think in absolute terms makes it hard for the pre-operational child to see objects in relation to each other. He may have difficulties when it comes to putting objects accurately into any ordered sequence, or making distinctions between different kinds of categories. Thus if a group consisted of four girls and six boys, and a pre-operational child is asked 'Are there more boys or more children in this group?', he is likely to answer, 'More boys.' Similarly, a child at this age may find it hard to categorize objects consistently. Asked to sort a group of different objects into two types, he may choose an arbitrary distinction, such as colour, to separate them, even when the introduction of a third colour has made nonsense of the categorization, which should in fact have proceeded according to some more subtle cue such as shape. A child at the level of concrete operations may be able to change his strategy at this point, taking account of this new factor of a third colour; a pre-operational child may simply soldier on, less and less logically.

There are other characteristics of operational thinking that one could mention, but perhaps by now its essential character and importance are becoming clear. Operational thinking enables a child to become more objective about his egocentric impressions, to understand relations between things and to categorize objects more logically. When a child is able to organize his perceptions in this more rational way, he is on the way to possessing a coherent intellectual system – very different from his earlier intuitive thinking.

THE IMPORTANCE OF THE LEVEL OF CONCRETE OPERATIONS

Whereas formal operational thinking is only found where there is a certain kind of education, most human societies seem to reach a level of concrete operations. Only in certain hunter-gatherer societies do individuals never seem to grow out of the pre-operational stage. Children in various societies and from different social backgrounds may differ in the intellectual area in which they first attain the concept of conservation: Barbara Lloyd points out that sons of potters in Mexico, for example, understand the conservation of substance earlier than children of parents in other crafts.[17] But it should not be assumed that once the idea of conservation has been grasped in one area, it will necessarily be applied to all the child's thinking. He may understand the conservation of quantity (e.g. of objects) as early as six years old, but it may take another five years before the concept of the conservation of *volume* (e.g. of clay or water) is fully appreciated. Certainly by the age of eight or so, most children will realize that the amount of water does not change when it is poured from a short fat container into a long thin one. But it may take another three years for them to work from this to the idea that the short fat flask and the tall thin one, if the same amount of water fills both to the brim, must necessarily be exactly alike in capacity, or volume.

Nevertheless, the striking fact remains that concrete operational thinking occurs in nearly all human societies, and its attainment does not necessarily depend upon any formal education. According to David Elkind: 'Children in bush Africa, Hong Kong and Appalachia all attain concrete operations at about the same ages as middle-class children in Geneva and Boston.'[18] Some recent attempts to speed up the transition to concrete operational thought through a specially devised educational syllabus have not been impressive. Quite how children come to make this transition in thinking style remains an open question, but it almost certainly depends upon an interaction between environmental stimulation, previous experience and physiological development. J. M. Tanner, for example, considers that Piaget's successive stages probably depend to a large extent upon the progressive maturation and organization of that part of the brain known as the cortex, although he also allows that 'without at least some degree of social stimulus the latent abilities may never be exercised'.[19]

This might explain why it is so difficult to teach operational thinking to children before they are intellectually ready for it. It also suggests why, once children have attained the concept of conservation, it is then very difficult to persuade them from it. A Norwegian psychologist, Jan Smedslund, tried setting up an experimental situation which by trickery appeared to contradict the fact of conservation. Two equal lumps of plasticine were shown to the child, one was then altered radically in shape, and the child was then asked to predict whether it would still weigh the same or not. The child was required to test his prediction by weighing the two quantities of plasticine on a scale balance. But surreptitiously the experimenter stole some plasticine from the total amount as he changed its shape, so that it did in fact weigh less on the scales. Children who hadm erely been coached into ideas of quantity conservation before the experiment quickly reverted to pre-conservation notions – this proved, for them, that somehow changing the shape of the plasticine had changed its weight. But children who had already arrived at the concept of conservation by themselves, and who had no need of previous coaching, simply would not accept what was going on, correctly insisting that there must be some mistake or trick.[20] In this way, operational thinking – once it has been acquired – seems to have some of the force of an organized intellectual system that cannot simply be unlearned – unlike a more isolated piece of knowledge which would not necessarily be bound up with a whole new style of thinking. This again suggests that the process is accompanied by a maturing of the nervous system which enables a child to reason like this – in a way that would not have been possible, except superficially, at an earlier stage.

Could it be that the attainment of operational thinking plays a universal part in definitions of childhood? Time and again in history one finds cases where the adult world has drawn a distinction between the younger child, with his predilection for play and general lack of real understanding, and the older youth, who is thought to have attained an age of reason and is therefore more responsible for his actions. This is well illustrated in a story about the young Moses, not quoted in the

Bible but found in the Talmud:

> About this time, when Moses was three years old, Pharaoh,
> sitting at his banquet table, with his queen upon his right,
> Bathia at his left, and his two sons, with Bil'am and the
> princes of his realm about him, took Moses upon his lap.
> The child stretched forth his hand, and taking the royal
> crown from Pharaoh's head placed it upon his own.
> In this action the king and the people around him imagined
> they saw a meaning, and Pharaoh asked:
> 'How shall this Hebrew boy be punished?'
> Then said Bil'am, the son of Be'or, the magician, 'Think
> not, because the child is young, that he did this thing
> thoughtlessly . . .'
> When the judges and wise men assembled according to
> the order of the king, Jithro, the priest of Midian, came with
> them. The king related the child's action and the advice
> which Bil'am had given him, requesting their opinions on the
> same.
> Then said Jithro, desirous to preserve the child's life:
> 'If it be pleasing to the king, let two plates be placed before
> the child, one containing fire, the other gold. If the child
> stretches forth his hand to grasp the gold, we will know him
> to be an understanding being, and consider that he acted
> towards thee knowingly, deserving death. But if he grasps the
> fire, let his life be spared.'
> This advice met with the king's approval, and two plates,
> one containing gold, the other fire, were placed before the
> infant Moses. The child put forth his hand, and grasping
> the fire put it to his mouth, burning his tongue, and becoming
> thereafter 'heavy of mouth and heavy of tongue', as men-
> tioned in the Bible. Through this childish action the life of
> Moses was saved.

Here, the distinction between two levels of childhood is
clearly made, in terms of an immature response to the more
immediately attractive but dangerous fire, or a responsible
reaction to the less enticing but more valuable gold. There
are many other examples of adults seeing childhood as defined
by some cut-off point in the ability to understand. Throughout his book, Ariès emphasizes the significance attributed to

the age of seven in France in the sixteenth century and before. For many adults seven seemed to mark the beginning of some sort of age of reason; before that, as in one medieval text quoted by Ariès, 'That which is born is called an infant, which is as good as saying not talking, because in this age it cannot talk well or form its words perfectly, for its teeth are not yet well arranged or firmly implanted.' And elsewhere too, children under seven seem to have been considered good only for playing games, and as 'not worth much when all is told'. This boundary may have originated in Roman law, which was later absorbed into most North European legal systems. According to that, children under seven were legally *infantia*, and then until puberty (fixed at the age of fourteen for boys, and twelve for girls) *tutela impuberes*. In England, as late as the eighteenth century, a child once over the age of seven was held responsible for his crimes: in one typical case a small girl aged seven was hanged in the Market Place in Norwich for stealing a petticoat.[21] Bearing in mind the importance this age always seems to have had in adults' perception of children, is it co-incidence that Piaget has found that most children do indeed start showing evidence of early operational thinking at around this time?

There are also legions of affectionate stories throughout history of younger children saying the wrong thing at the wrong time or, in Piagetian terms, showing their powers of assimilating adult ways and phrases, while still unable to accommodate them into a correct context of behaviour. 'When little children are caught in a trap, when they say something foolish, drawing a correct inference from an irrelevant principle which has been given to them, people burst out laughing, rejoice at having tricked them, or kiss and caress them as if they had worked out the correct answer.'[22] This irritable complaint by Fleury, a seventeenth-century peda-gogue, obviously refers to those little stories that were later to become so popular in the pages of *Punch* during the nine-teenth century, or in small collections often edited by prosper-ous ladies, of children's artless and occasionally artful remarks. To quote a typical social 'howler':

Child: 'Do you eat hay?'
Guest: 'No; why do you ask?'
Child: 'Because Mummy says you eat like a horse.'

There can, of course, be more delicate shades of misunderstanding, where it is only the social significance of certain phrases, and not their literal meaning, that is misunderstood. Molly Weir recalls:

Once I got carried away by what I thought was Grannie's praise of a chum's mother who had a particularly explosive laugh. I burst out admiringly, 'Oh, Mrs D., laugh like that again. My Grannie says you've a laugh like a hen cackling.' Grannie seized me by the ear the minute I came in from play and demanded to know why I'd been so silly as to cause trouble like this, for of course Mrs D. had been furious. Somehow I just couldn't make Grannie understand that I thought it was a compliment. If I had been able to laugh like a hen cackling I'd have been delighted with my cleverness.[23]

In another context, children's tactless honesty has been seen as admirable, especially when it punctuates pomposity or justifiably passes on home truths, as in Hans Andersen's *The emperor's new clothes*.

Obviously children may also make awkward remarks after the age of seven and the onset of operational thinking, but by and large I would suggest that most societies distinguish between children before what is often loosely thought of as the beginning of reason, around seven or so, and afterwards, when more is expected, and when formal education has often started. Such a distinction will not be a hard and fast one, but it may partly rest on the perception of differences between pre-operational and later thinking. A pre-operational child, as we have seen, is more inclined to believe in surface appearances; his concentration span is shorter, his perception of cause and effect limited, and his ability to learn from other people's experience small. If he walks away from home he may not be able to find his way back, unless he is in very familiar surroundings. Unlike an older child, he may not be capable of forming or retaining a mental image of the series of actions or decisions that are required in following a new route. When he tries to classify objects, he may put them together in an arbitrary, subjective manner. A big coin may seem to be worth more than a small one, simply because of its superior size, and an older child may be able to cheat him out of, say, an expensive wristwatch by offering in exchange a wooden catapult. For a younger child, both objects may simply be toys, and the catapult if anything more desirable.

An inability to judge accurately between appearance and reality, to see the underlying significance of one's own or other people's actions, to spot significant relationships, or to have any reliable concept of number, will always to a certain extent make the pre-operational child inferior to and dependent on adults and older children. It will also limit his usefulness in work situations demanding concentration, or logical or sequential thinking. I suggest, therefore, that most societies in some senses recognize the pre-operational stage and make allowances for it. Naturally, though, when a child has attained operational thinking he does not immediately become an adult; in a developed society this may have to wait for mastery of formal operational thinking after a great deal more education. But when a child is at the stage of concrete operations, he will certainly be on something closer to an equal footing with the adults around him, especially in a simple society where the basic techniques of handicraft and agriculture may not call for more than this level of intellect.

CAN CHILDREN'S INTELLECTUAL DEVELOPMENT BE SPEEDED UP?

There are other important ways in which children can be distinguished from adults, but different intellectual levels and styles do seem to provide one useful means of defining the child in diverse societies. The distinction may mean very little when we are faced by a child prodigy who can think like an adult, and inevitably it is stories of children such as these that have been most popular throughout history. Records of the intellectual development of normal children, at least outside the schoolroom, are harder to find.

Sometimes, however, a society has put a high premium on early education. This happened in Elizabethan and Stuart England when the Renaissance created general respect for learning. At that time, children might be expected to read Latin and Greek at the age of five, and many – with parents who could afford it – seemed to have achieved high educational standards at this early age. Does this sort of evidence contradict what we asserted previously, that stages of intellectual growth cannot be hurried by intensive teaching? Or is it that all children are naturally disposed to learn languages anyway, and have good powers of rote memory at an early age? Is this what the Elizabethans built upon in such early education? Whether such infants also showed early analytic skills as well, and were able to reason abstractly in advance of their twentieth-century counterparts, we really cannot assess.

On the other hand, there is new evidence that the ages which Piaget tentatively put forward as 'norms' for attaining the various stages of mental growth may indeed vary. Other psychologists maintain that when presented with carefully modified versions of some of the experimental situations originally set by Piaget, children can respond to them more logically than Piaget himself would once have thought likely or even possible.[24] This might support the idea that the timing of the acquisition of such stages is still not really well understood.

Certain parents throughout history have set out to push their children's intellects as hard as they can, sometimes with marked success. The eighteenth-century Dr Malkin, for example, described his sons as 'linguists at 3, profound philosophers at 5, read the Fathers at 6'.[25] But again one would like to know what he meant by a 'philosopher'. Yet it could also be argued that no one today, not even a psychologist anxious to prove an experiment with his own children, would ever dare push his infants quite as hard as the Elizabethans did, with long hours of study and frequent beatings. So the exact effect of such forcible feeding on the earlier development of intellectual skills must in some ways remain an open question – but an important one, which I shall discuss further in the final chapter. Whatever the possible variation in age for the attainment of Piaget's intellectual stages, there is considerable cross-cultural evidence that individual intellectual development does follow the sequence he suggests.

CONCLUSIONS

In fact – as will have been clear – much of the argument in this chapter rests on Piaget's experiments and theories. In a new science like psychology it would be optimistic to hope for a developmental theory on which every psychologist could agree but, though Piaget's ideas have been modified in detail over the last fifty years, they still hold together most successfully, and in broad outline have provided researchers in European and other cultures with scientific facts that on the whole have been confirmed by further experiments. Piaget has provided the only complete theory of intellectual development at present available; no other theory covers such a broad area in so much detail. It has not been possible in the space available to consider different explanations of human intellectual development, but Piaget in my opinion still offers the best and most comprehensive guide to these processes, and can throw most light on any search for common psychological factors in children.

But does Piaget, even so, tend to concentrate too much on a special kind of child – European or American, middle-class, and used to ordering his own environment? Jerome Bruner, for example, has drawn attention to the way in which very impoverished children in America and elsewhere develop linguistically and intellectually. For a child born in a culture where there is a general feeling of hopelessness and ineffectiveness, there may be less stimulation to achieve that mastery over the environment that is so central to Piaget's theories. Jerome Bruner again:

> Quite possibly it is only the 'powerful', well-cared for, competent child who sees the world in the pattern of his own feelings, and not the malnourished child of many traditional

subsistence cultures . . . It may be that a collective, rather than individual, value orientation develops where the individual lacks power over the physical world. Lacking personal power, he has no notion of personal importance. In terms of his cognitive categories, now, he will be less likely to set himself apart from others. [26]

This recalls Burckhardt's comment about the Middle Ages: 'Man was conscious of himself only as a member of a race, people, party, family or corporation – only through some general category.' In this sense, an inability to distinguish between the inner and the outer world is certainly not something always confined to young children.

We have already pointed out that unfavourable environmental conditions, whether malnutrition or lack of stimulation, can indeed stunt children in various ways. Such conditions were widespread in the past and still are in some underdeveloped countries today. Even so, for a psychologist like Piaget who works from a biological point of view, it makes more sense to study an organism which is functioning in optimum conditions – which in the case of the child implies a certain level of food, stimulation and emotional security. Given these, Piaget's theories are a reliable guide. They can at least help us understand children living in other than very straitened circumstances.

The conclusions of this chapter, that, other things being equal, young children think in a different style from older children and adults, may not seem revolutionary. Yet clarifying such differences has not always proved easy, and putting them into the context of a universal developmental scheme may help us to make clearer generalizations about children and adults in the future.

5/Summing up:
what is a child?

So far we have looked at the child from four different but related viewpoints, and tried to establish certain constant features in a picture that varies widely over time and space.

Socially, the child is receptive to the different biases of the culture he is born into, and the particular ways in which these are transmitted to him by his parents or caregivers. Because of this, any search for the 'natural child', over and above the minimum common ground, faces difficulties. There is, for example, widespread evidence that marked individual differences exist, possibly relating to genetic inheritance, body type and basic personality structure. But perhaps even more importantly, childhood is so much – though not entirely – a function of adult expectations and practices that it will always reflect differences between cultures, which may sometimes mask the essential similarities between all children. But receptivity to a prevailing culture is in itself a constant characteristic of all childhood. Children brought up without adult influences, as the so-called 'wild' or 'wolf' children were once thought to be, would in a sense be inhuman, lacking any of the socializing influence from an immediate social group that contributes so much to human nature itself. The very existence of 'wild' children brought up by animals and living apart from human civilization, is anyway now in doubt, and the whole idea seems to owe more to mythology than to scientific research. But children who have been abandoned in less romantic circumstances to live alone in extreme neglect over a number of years have had little that is human about them when they have been discovered, so far as capacity for speech, thought or feeling is concerned, although treatment has helped some to recover at least partly from this state.

Physically, the growing child is faced by certain physiological constraints that will limit what he can do; otherwise, his general development of motor skills tends to follow a fairly predictable path. His sexual immaturity puts him in a different category from adults, although societies may interpret this distinction in different ways.

Emotionally, all young children soon learn to attach themselves to a limited number of more mature figures, and at certain times show fear of strangers outside this select group, but different societies react differently to this behaviour. All children seem to experience fear at certain common situations or fantasies, but they also appear to derive pleasure from exploring the world around them, very often through the medium of play. Later, the growing child will normally become interested in the activities of others, especially his own contemporaries. Growth towards sexual and intellectual maturity sometimes seems to face children with emotional problems. If these are not resolved, the individual's personality and self-confidence may suffer as a result, although it is not clear whether such emotional crises – for example, around puberty – in an individual's life history occur universally, or chiefly in more complex societies which stress the importance of the individual rather than that of the total, inclusive community.

Intellectually, the child seems to develop certain cognitive skills at predictable stages. In the course of this process of intellectual development the younger child is particularly at the mercy of his immediate perceptions, as he is unable to base his understanding on considerations other than the here-and-now. Later, his thinking will approximate more closely to adult thought, although he may never attain powers of abstract thought without formal education.

CHILDHOOD: APPRENTICESHIP
TO SOCIETY   *A changes depending on Culture*

In a way, the idea of a genuinely child-centred culture is nonsense: childhood is a period where the individual learns about the total, adult environment that he has been born into, and where he prepares himself for his own place within it. In a poor society like the Mexican slums, the need to get children wage-earning as quickly as possible means that 'On the family level the major traits of the culture of poverty are the absence of childhood as a specially prolonged and protected stage in the life cycle'.[1] In two highly developed societies, such as the USA and the USSR, childhood experience again differs in a number of ways, reflecting the contrasting values of each country. Children in Russia are accustomed, from a very early age, to spend a large part of the day in the company of their peers. At school constant stress is laid on loyalty to the group; which in turn is heavily influenced by the norms set for it by the teacher, which reflect the basic ideals of Soviet society itself. In this situation it is quite common to find a striking uniformity of belief and behaviour in the young all over Russia. In America, the emphasis seems more on the individuality of the child and the socializing effect of the peer group, in itself much less under the influence of adult leadership and conscious norms of 'correct' behaviour.[2] It would be rash for any critic to contend that one regime is more 'natural' than the other. Everyone may have their own preferences, but so far as the children themselves are concerned, they will soon feel most at home in the type of system they have become socialized into, and which is an appropriate preparation for the lives they are going to lead as adults.

This is not quite to say that children will necessarily flourish under any form of socialization, however much it cuts across the common needs and characteristics of childhood that there are. All humans have a large capacity for adaptation, especially when very young, yet in a situation such as Wesley's school which denied children so much, it may eventually have to be the system that changes. Even so, there is plenty of evidence that children in the past have been forced to accept, and have eventually become used to, quite appalling conditions in homes, schools or places of work. Writing about some elderly informants who were questioned recently about their childhoods in Britain at the turn of the century, Paul Thompson points out that it is 'striking how few children recall any systematic challenge to their parents' authority at this stage. Even among those children who remember disliking or indeed hating drunken parents, stories of resistance are rare.'[3] Dr Thompson ascribes this lack of domestic resistance to children's essential 'age-mobility'. 'Solidarity can scarcely be learnt before the leader of resistance joins the oppressors with the rest of his peer group. Women's liberation at least does not suffer from the devastating handicap that all women will in time become men.' And one can add to this the very obvious point made before, that children are on the whole smaller and weaker than adults, and economically, socially and even emotionally very heavily dependent upon those who can impose such intolerable conditions upon them.

It is not surprising, therefore, that while there are numerous and largely predictable similarities between babies the whole world over, these decline as children grow older and increasingly adapt themselves to the modes and customs of their own societies. As Piaget puts it, 'Childhood . . . is a biologically useful phase whose significance is that of a progressive adaptation to a physical and social environment.'[4] Social critics over the years have had various ideas as to what childhood *ought* to consist of, but in order to change particular childhood patterns one must first change the society that produces the children. Sometimes early childhood has been regarded as an idyllic time of innocence, before education or other social pressures have had a chance to push the child into artificial kinds of behaviour, possibly antithetical to his supposedly 'real' nature. But childhood is a period where the individual is adapting himself to the environment all the time; there is no way in which a child can defer this process, although in more complex societies there may be an increased choice of models of behaviour for him to follow. The notion that one can somehow stay as a child, impervious to the demands of one's own surroundings as one grows older, ignores the essentially adaptive nature of childhood, or indeed of man at any age.

Nevertheless, various concepts of childhood have often been used by critics to attack what they see as the constraints or evils of adult society. Children, like Noble Savages, have symbolically peopled an ideal state, eventually to be corrupted by the artificial demands of 'civilization'. Certainly, in many societies children are allowed freedoms denied to adults. Some of these freedoms may seem part of the nature of childhood itself – spontaneous, improvised play, for example. Others, such as the general prohibition in the Western world on young children working full-time for money, may result from a history of legislation. In this sense, childhood already shares a great deal of the 'artificiality' that so many critics have seen as applying only to adult society.

Looking at what passes for childhood in Western Europe and America today, we can see that the dividing line between 'childish' and 'adult' behaviour is constantly being redrawn both in minor and major ways, so emphasizing the essentially relative and social nature of these terms. In the early nineteenth century, for example, it was quite permissible for an adult to shed copious tears in public: readings by Charles Dickens from his own works used to release floods of emotion, and even in Parliament, 'as late as 1815, Creevey was relating that "there was not a dry eye in the House . . . Tierney sobbed so, he was unable to speak; I never saw a more affecting scene".' During the same period, adults would read fairy stories and the nonsense of Edward Lear along with their children, and the audience for Punch and Judy shows would consist of people of all ages; it was only by the end of the nineteenth century that children would make up practically the whole crowd. None of this, except in unusual circumstances, would be considered adult behaviour today, even though it passed without comment such a short time ago.

Adults have sometimes regretted fundamental intellectual and emotional changes undergone since childhood – a time, for Wordsworth in 'Ode: Intimations of Immortality',

> When meadow, grove, and stream,
> The earth, and every common sight,
> To me did seem
> Apparelled in celestial light,
> The glory and the freshness of a dream.

Certainly, familiar objects and sensations may possess a novelty and excitement for children which are more difficult to catch later when we become habituated to such things. For an artist, a vision of this type may never recur so intensely in later life. It is not surprising that Wordsworth in particular mourned the process by which we become divorced by age from the feelings and perceptions of childhood. His own poetic vision of nature always seemed to derive much of its inspiration from memories of the essentially animistic way in which a child may look upon the outside world at certain early stages. The 'pathetic fallacy', whereby some writers self-consciously attribute feelings and characters to trees, mountains, lakes or whatever in their poetry or prose, may be a reality to the younger child, who may look upon his environment in this more personalized, emotional way as a matter of course.

Wordsworth also appeared to recognize that there were some compensations in growing older – when he came to write 'Tintern Abbey', a type of mysticism seems to compensate for the loss of his earlier, more immediate reactions:

> other gifts
> Have followed; for such a loss, I would believe,
> Abundant recompense. For I have learned
> To look on nature, not as in the hour
> Of thoughtless youth; but hearing oftentimes
> The still, sad music of humanity.

Regret for losing some of the pleasures of childhood is one thing, but to make a cult of immaturity, as some of the works of J. M. Barrie do, is a denial of adulthood as much as an exaltation of childhood, open to the sort of scolding once handed out by T. S. Eliot when reviewing a book on the poetry of Henry Vaughan (who was, in fact, a most moving poet on the theme of childhood):

> This love of one's own childhood . . . is anything but a token of greatness. We all know the mood; and we can all, if we choose to relax to that extent, indulge in the luxury of reminiscence of childhood; but if we are at all mature and conscious, we refuse to indulge this weakness to the point of writing or poetizing about it; we know that it is something to be buried and done with.[5]

THE PRESENT AND THE FUTURE

Changing trends in our own time, some bringing the child and adult closer together, others forcing them further apart, make any predictions about future patterns of childhood extremely tentative. On the one hand, longer periods of education are prolonging children's dependent status, yet the intellectual gap between an educated adult and a child is now so enormous that only increasingly sophisticated educational systems can enable the child to bridge it. The spread of higher education in the Western world, and the increasing technical complexity of so much adult work, has thus exaggerated the intellectual differences that have always existed between children and adults, although usually in rather less distinctive ways. Even at the beginning of this century it was still possible for an intelligent child, reading one of the great popularizers such as H. G. Wells, to gain quite a shrewd idea of what was going on in the higher regions of science. A young historian, similarly, might find himself sharing the obvious patriotism of a popular historian without any difficulty. Now, the scientist has taken off into a world where few colleagues outside his speciality, let alone schoolchildren, can follow him, while the historian has developed new research techniques and a more quizzical attitude towards his material than most younger readers would be prepared to follow or understand. Even in popular fiction, while there are still novelists who are read by all ages, the tendency is again increasingly for the

Not recent but has become more significant.

field to break down into specifically directed adult or child reading.

At work, the gulf between adult and child is also greater than ever before. Occupations where son works alongside father, learning as he goes, are increasingly replaced by jobs which require a basic technical training. Opportunities for a boy to learn a man's job by observing adults around him and sometimes joining in become fewer every year, as workers move from the countryside into towns, and work itself becomes hidden away in separate and impenetrable institutions.

This change in the status of childhood is particularly important for girls; looking at the history of childhood, it is striking how much, in the past, reference has been made to boys alone. In the gradual separation between child and adult life styles, it was in general boys who first received organized education, had toys made for them, and were expected to exhibit the type of noisy, boisterous behaviour of the very young. For girls, particularly from poorer homes, childhood often had to compete with growing domestic responsibilities, which might put them in charge of the younger ones during the mother's succeeding confinements. Girls from very early on would model themselves on their mothers, and sometimes the fit would be a close one indeed. Today, however, when girls more frequently stay on at school and face a wider choice of possible adult roles than ever before, the situation can be very different. Like their brothers, girls too may now appear to prolong their childhoods by not taking on adult, maternal roles at an early age, and by keeping their options open during increasingly long periods of education and dependence.

In many ways there is a greater division between adults and children today than before, now that children are segregated into educational institutions for long periods, with less opportunity to share in adult work. On the other hand, one can also point to a relaxation of former boundaries between the ages. Relationships tend to be easier today, with less formality than was once expected when a child addressed an adult (given that he was permitted to do such a thing without prior assent).

The distinction between adults & children lost again ⇒ in a different way to Aries' suggestion.

Summing up: what is a child? 107

Now one can hear children refer to adults by their christian names, and at home parents and children will eat together and watch the same television programmes. Discussion about domestic matters may now proceed on a more equal basis, with the whole family joining in to make decisions. Children are also less protected now from discussion about once-taboo subjects, particularly sex, and their own behaviour in this and other areas may proceed with less attempted adult supervision and censure than before.

At the same time, typically childish clothes – the sailor suits and frilly dresses of affluent children in former times – are giving way to more adult fashions at increasingly early stages in a child's life. Soon it may only be the baby in the first year who has his own distinctive outfit. Food shows a similar lack of differentiation: previously the diet thought suitable for children (and often servants too) was often a very plain one: milk and suet puddings, for example, and generally a lack of protein. John Locke, among many other writers who throughout history were forever warning parents against rich food for the young, recommended that all 'flesh' should be avoided until the child was six or seven; he thought the ideal diet before that consisted of milk, fruit, brown bread and gruel. Even as late as 1930 it was possible to find books on child-rearing that ruled out meat for babies under two, and in one case, for any child under ten. Today, it would be harder to distinguish between the diet of an adult and that of any child no longer a baby. Curiously, the elaborate cakes and individual jellies that once were common, along with fancy dress and party games, in adult parties, and which then became more associated with childhood gatherings, now show signs of being dropped by children too. At the birthday party of a modern, Western child, there may now be savoury food and pop music rather than sweet foods and nursery rhymes. This pattern by which children take over sections of adult behaviour is familiar; it applies as well to games, slang and jokes.

Where these sometimes contradictory pressures leave children today is a matter for argument. Life may indeed be more clearcut in simple societies, which may lack the inconsistent and unpredictable patterns of dependence and independence presented to the young in our own culture. But given that our society must spend a great deal of time on the education of its young, in order to provide the skilled labour force necessary for its maintenance, then a long period of adolescence – where the individual is neither child nor adult – may be an inevitable result. It is one explanation for the rise of a 'youth culture' which may help to buttress a young person through this confusing period.   → aft childhood & bt adulthood.

CAN WE ANSWER THE QUESTION 'WHAT IS A CHILD?'?

If we have not been able to produce an exact concept of the natural child in this and the preceding chapters, I hope nevertheless that some common characteristics have become clear. With such a formidable field of evidence one has to beware both of being too tentative, and of being too specific. (In all areas of psychology, there is the risk that readers will treat hypotheses and generalized findings as hard facts, applying them in every case to their own children. This was often the way with the series of behavioural norms worked out by Arnold Gesell in his lifelong work studying cross-sections of American children in order to establish the usual age for the onset of particular interests or activities. Parents would wonder why their infant was not standing up at such and such a month, or why their older boy was not cracking the sort of jokes typical, say, of the mid-years of childhood.) Psychology deals more with probabilities than certainties, and most findings about norms in human nature can never hope to cover the range of individual differences and variations in behaviour.

It will be obvious that a number of really fundamental questions about childhood have still to be answered, either because there is not enough evidence, or perhaps because the questions are unanswerable. It is still not clear, for instance, to what extent some of the intellectual and social processes associated with children's development can be speeded up. In what sense, for example, would a little factory hand of the nineteenth century be recognized as a child today? Certainly, he would have had to adapt to the hideous reality of an adult world very quickly, or simply not survive. If his mastery of experience, in this way, was an adult one, in what other ways would he have remained childish? Intellectually he may have had much in common with the uneducated adults around him; what his emotions may have been, one can simply never know.

At the other end of the social scale, consider J. H. van den Berg's description of some of the precocious, and to our eyes overeducated, children of seventeenth- and eighteenth-century Europe.

> The precociousness of talented children in earlier days is astonishing to us ... Goethe, for instance, was able to write German, French, Greek and Latin before he was eight. He picked up Italian while his father was teaching this language to his little seven-year-old sister ... The Jesuit monk, Père Joseph (1597), recited the drama of Golgotha, standing on his own little table at a dinner party given by his father, when he was four years old. A Dutch commander of a company of infantry, Menno van Coehoom, was sixteen years old when he was transferred from Friesland to a garrison in Maastricht. And so on – an almost endless series of precocious children, children who evidently at a very young age were considered able enough to go to a university and who appeared capable of digesting the very mature matters offered to them. If a girl were educated at all, she too started when she was two or three years old.[6]

Now Dr van den Berg is a psychologist, not a historian, and one would like to know more about his claim for an 'endless series of precocious children'. Goethe is hardly a fair example of what can be done with a normal child; how many other of these prodigies may have been in fact the geniuses to whom no rules of development would easily apply? There is some suggestion, too, that these child prodigies, far from constituting some type of educational norm, as Dr van den Berg appears to suggest, were viewed – and sometimes resented – as something

quite extraordinary even then. 'Endeavouring to make
children prematurely wise', lectured Dr Johnson,

> is useless labour. Suppose they have more knowledge at five
> or six years old than other children, what use can be made of
> it? It will be lost before it is wanted, and the waste of so
> much time and labour of the teacher can never be repaid.
> Too much is expected from precocity, and too little performed.
> Miss Aikin was an instance of early cultivation, but in what
> did it terminate? In marrying a little Presbyterian parson, who
> keeps an infant boarding school.[7]

On the other hand, there is ample evidence that the demands upon children who received formal education at that
time could be very stringent; Rousseau complained about it
strongly in *Émile*, where he attacked the premature treatment
of children as adults. One of his early followers, J. H. Campe,
made the same point in 1786. He found it disturbing to meet
an eight- or ten-year-old boy

> who has read a whole library of books, who can converse
> about the plants and animals of India, who speaks many
> languages, who knows all the paradigmata of Latin grammar
> by heart, who calculates like a merchant and who explains
> the classical authors with an ability which brings tears of joy
> to every true schoolmaster's eyes.[8]

Rousseau and Campe were attacking what was fairly
orthodox educational practice at the time. They may have been
exaggerating its effects, but even if this were so, one can still
concede a further point to Dr van den Berg. 'What about the
great men of our day? If they are like the talented of the past,
they too should have been precocious. There is no evidence of
this. The youth of those who in our own century have been
scientific pioneers cannot stand comparison with d'Aubigné,
Pascal, Grotius or Goethe.' There is exaggeration here too:
distinguished men of our own century have quite frequently
shown an unusual talent while still at school. But Dr van den
Berg is right to insist that in most cases this show of talent
does not measure up to that of some of the prodigies found in
the past.

In fact, there is probably enough contemporary evidence available to suggest that if very intense educational pressure is imposed upon children by parents or tutors working outside the normal educational system, then they may resemble precocious children from the seventeenth or eighteenth centuries. In the United States, for example, one mother this century raised her daughter according to the following rather eccentric regime. At six weeks she began by reciting *Horatius at the bridge* over the cot, which made the baby, we are told, kick her feet and wave her hands.[9] Later, she would put her baby to sleep, scanning portions of the *Aeneid* aloud meanwhile. She also taught the 'black mammy' in charge of the child to recite the first ten lines of Book I on those occasions when she herself was absent. When the baby developed control of her limbs, the classics were again brought into service, this time for Mrs Stoner's especially invented game of 'Virgil-ball', where the mother and child would roll a ball to each other at every other word.

After so much effort, it is almost a relief to report that the child did show the hoped-for signs of precocity, using a typewriter at the age of three, and mastering eight languages, so we are told, at five years old. A somewhat similar picture is presented in *The Children on the Hill*, a more recent account of a family living in Wales where the mother did all the house-work at night in order to devote herself exclusively to her children's education during the day. Sure enough, the oldest child went on to show outstanding mathematical ability for his age, another was a promising pianist, and a third had an IQ of the highest possible score.

It would therefore seem that children can be pushed very much beyond the normal educational attainments found in Western schools at the moment, and that the pace at which intellectual growth proceeds does seem to depend in some ways upon the child's environment. This makes 'natural' educational growth a more relative matter than is sometimes supposed. Yet if we were to push all children much harder, it could still be argued that they might suffer through a dis-tortion of their overall development in other important ways.

John Stuart Mill, who knew his Greek alphabet at three and could correct his elders in this and in Latin at five, also recorded, in his very moving autobiography, a childhood virtually without play, and an adulthood that was far from happy. There are also suggestions, in *The Children on the Hill*, of quite marked social difficulties in at least one of the children.[10] Educationalists who recommend taking some formal educational pressure off young pupils can make a case that children need the time saved to learn other non-educational skills equally important for their all-round development.

This type of argument can never be resolved; the most 'natural' child and the most 'natural' environment must remain matters of opinion. It does seem clear, however, as Jerome Bruner says, that 'some environments "push" cognitive growth better, earlier, and longer than others. What does not seem to happen is that different cultures produce completely divergent and unrelated modes of thought. The reason for this must be the constraint of our biological heritage.'[11]

Lastly, we must return to one of the most fundamental arguments about children, with which we started this book. What are the respective weightings of nature as against nurture in a child's moral character and development? Religion has always concerned itself with this problem. For John Milton, and most other Christians of the time of *Paradise Lost*, children were the direct inheritors of man's original sin, the result

> Of Man's first disobedience, and the fruit
> Of that forbidden tree, whose mortal taste
> Brought death into the world, and all our woe,
> With loss of Eden.

At around the same time, a rather different point of view could also sometimes be heard, at first put forward tentatively, but later with more confidence. In 1628 John Earle could write in his *Microcosmography* 'A child is a man in a small letter, yet the best copy of Adam before he tasted of Eve or the apple . . . His soul is yet a white paper unscribbled with observations of the world . . . he knows no evil.' The most famous exponent of this particular notion was of course John Locke, who described the infant mind in 1699 as a *tabula rasa* – a blank sheet that would eventually be filled by accumulated education and experience. This idea of the child as at least morally neutral at birth, rather than conceived and born in sin, was taken much further by Rousseau. His *Émile* is still the most powerful argument in favour of the child as born with an innate sense of goodness, able to develop harmoniously and without the need for excessive adult supervision, through adaptation to the natural environment around him. This view was later taken even further by many others, particularly early educationists such as Pestalozzi, and it can still be recognized in educational theory today, for example in the work of Montessori or A. S. Neill.

In our own century, psychologists have increasingly contributed to this discussion. For Freud, man was born with certain instincts and racial memories that he can ignore only at peril; in *Civilization and its Discontents* he pictures society as perpetually at war with the more destructive, aggressive instincts of man, which at best can only lead to a state of continual tension and repression, both in the individual and within his culture. From an utterly different standpoint, an early behavioural psychologist like J. B. Watson could write, 'Give me a dozen healthy infants, well-formed and my own specified world to bring them up in and I'll guarantee to take any one at random and train him to become any type of specialist I might select – doctor, lawyer, artist, merchant-chief, and yes, even beggarman and thief, regardless of his talents, penchants, tendencies, abilities, vocations, and race of his ancestors.'[12] In this brave new world, the experimenter can apparently produce, via the conditioned reflex, almost any emotions or behaviour in children that he desires.

Modern psychologists almost always take up less extreme positions in this argument, and would probably find themselves somewhere midway between the two points of view. But to state that one believes in the necessary interaction of both

nature and nurture is still to beg a number of questions.
What sort of nature? What are the limits to the effects of
particular kinds of nurture? Ultimately, as we have said before,
to understand the exact balance and nature of these two forces
would be to understand man himself. Many claims have been
made for psychology in this century, but only an extremist
would state that anything like a complete synthesis of man has
as yet been put forward. Until this happens, children – like
adults – will never be completely understood.

Even so, if the moral core of man – or the child – is to
remain something of a mystery, the techniques by which both
parties set about organizing themselves and interacting with
their environment are now surely much better understood.
There are both similarities and differences between the various
ways in which adults and children do this. As Piaget has
written, 'The intellectual and moral structures of the child are
not the same as ours', and much of the argument of this book
has been devoted to making this point clearer, using as many
different perspectives and examples of child behaviour as
possible. But this is not the whole story. Children after all
grow into adults; in many ways their goals will always remain
the same; along with all other living things that have to
achieve mastery over themselves and their physical world in
order to survive. In this sense, both adults and children
respond to the same sort of stimulation, although in ways that
may differ in detail according to their present endowment of
skills, knowledge and experience. It could be that further
study of this particular way and habit of responding may
eventually tell us more about the very essence of man – or
child – than can be gleaned from any of the other schools of
philosophy or psychology so briefly considered in the last few
pages. For the moment, however, perhaps we can leave the
last word with Piaget, which is only just, as he is the person
who has done most to throw light on this whole issue.

With regard to mental functioning, the child is in fact
identical with the adult; like the adult, he is an active being
whose action, controlled by the law of interest or need, is

incapable of working at full stretch if no appeal is made to the autonomous motive forces of that activity. Just as the tadpole already breathes, though with different organs from those of the frog, so the child acts like the adult, but employing a mentality whose structure varies according to the stages of its development.[13]

References

PREFACE AND ACKNOWLEDGEMENTS

1 J. J. Rousseau, *Émile*, trans. B. Foxley (London: Dent, 1911) p. 5.
2 J. Holt, *Escape from Childhood* (Harmondsworth: Penguin, 1975) pp. 15, 175–6.
3 C. B. Cox and R. Boyson (eds.), *Black Paper 1975* (London: Dent, 1975) p. 1.
4 G. O. Trevelyan, *Life and Letters of Lord Macaulay* (London: Nelson, 1908) p. 42.
5 R. Garnett, *Life of Thomas Carlyle* (London: Walter Scott, 1887) p. 13.
6 S. Butler, *The Way of All Flesh* (1903; Harmondsworth: Penguin, 1966) p. 124.
7 P. Ariès, *Centuries of Childhood* (London: Cape, 1962) p. 46.

I. CHILDHOOD IN DIFFERENT CULTURES

1 P. Berger and T. Luckmann, *The Social Construction of Reality: a treatise in the sociology of knowledge* (New York: Doubleday, 1967) p. 66.
2 P. Berger and T. Luckmann, *The Social Construction of Reality*, p. 83.
3 J. F. Kett, 'Adolescence and youth in nineteenth-century America' in T. K. Rabb and R. I. Rotberg (eds.), *The Family in History, Interdisciplinary Essays* (New York: Harper and Row, 1973) p. 98.
4 Quoted in I. Stickland, *The Voices of Children 1700–1914* (Oxford: Blackwell, 1973) p. 202.
5 J. Lawson, *A Man's Life* (London: Hodder and Stoughton, 1932) p. 111.
6 J. Lawson, *A Man's Life*, pp. 109–10.
7 P. Ariès, *Centuries of Childhood*, p. 125.
8 P. Ariès, *Centuries of Childhood*, p. 125.
9 P. Ariès, *Centuries of Childhood*, p. 64.
10 S. Millar, *The Psychology of Play* (Harmondsworth: Penguin, 1968) pp. 247–8.

11 *Fénelon on Education*, trans. H. C. Barnard (Cambridge: Cambridge University Press, 1966) p. 25.
12 N. Machiavelli, *Florentine History*, trans. W. K. Marriott (London: Dent, 1909) p. 360.
13 P. Ariès, *Centuries of Childhood*, p. 65.
14 P. Ariès, *Centuries of Childhood*, p. 68.
15 P. Ariès, *Centuries of Childhood*, p. 125.
16 Quoted in P. Horn, *The Victorian Country Child* (Kineton: Roundwood Press, 1974) p. 86.
17 C. Laye, *The African Child* (London: Fontana, 1959) p. 41.
18 D. Defoe, *A Tour thro' the Island of Great Britain 1724–7*, vol. 1 (London: Dent, 1962) p. 266.
19 P. Thompson, 'The war with adults,' *Oral History: the journal of the Oral History Society*, 1975, *3*, p. 30.
20 F. Thompson, *Lark Rise to Candleford* (London: Oxford University Press, 1945) pp. 450–1.
21 C. Laye, *The African Child*, p. 11.
22 C. Laye, *The African Child*, p. 15.
23 C. Laye, *The African Child*, p. 52.
24 Quoted in I. Stickland, *The Voices of Children 1700–1914* (Oxford: Blackwell, 1973) p. 102.
25 J. and E. Newson, *Seven Years Old in the Home Environment* (London: Allen and Unwin, 1976) p. 362.

2. GROWTH AND MATURITY

1 Quoted in L. de Mause (ed.), *The History of Childhood* (London: Souvenir Press, 1976) p. 118.
2 K. Danziger, *Socialization* (Harmondsworth: Penguin, 1971) pp. 144–5.
3 W. Dennis, 'Infant development under conditions of restricted practice and of minimum social stimulation,' *Genetic Psychology Monographs*, 1941, *23*, pp. 143–91.
4 W. Dennis, 'Causes of retardation among institutional children: Iran,' *Journal of Genetic Psychology*, 1960, *96*, pp. 47–59.
5 E. Pavenstedt, *The Drifters: children in disorganized lower class families* (London: Churchill, 1967).
6 See I. Eibl-Eibesfeldt, *Love and Hate: on the natural history of basic behaviour patterns* (London: Methuen, 1971) pp. 20–1.
7 M. Mead, *Male and Female* (London: Gollancz, 1949) p. 69.
8 I. Eibl–Eibesfeldt, *Love and Hate*.
9 Quoted in R. Blythe, *Akenfield* (London: Allen Lane, 1969) p. 88.
10 *Report of the Committee on the Age of Majority* (London: HMSO, 1967) p. 21.
11 M. K. Ashby, *Joseph Ashby of Tysoe 1859–1919* (Cambridge: Cambridge University Press, 1961) p. 39.

12 P. Ariès, *Centuries of Childhood*, p.103.
13 R. Benedict, 'Continuities and discontinuities in cultural conditioning' in M. Mead and M. Wolfenstein (eds.), *Childhood in Contemporary Cultures* (Chicago: University of Chicago Press, 1955) p. 27.

3. THE CHILD'S PERSONALITY

1 A. Hare, *The Story of My Life*, vol. 2 (London: George Allen 1896–1900), p. 93.
2 *The Essays of Montaigne*, vol. 1, trans. E. J. Trechmann (London: Oxford University Press, 1927) p. 390.
3 H. R. Schaffer, *The Growth of Sociability* (Harmondsworth: Penguin, 1971) p. 133.
4 M. Mead, 'A cultural anthropologist's approach to maternal deprivation' in *Deprivation of Maternal Care: a reassessment of its effects* (Geneva: World Health Organization, 1962).
5 J. Bowlby, *Attachment* (Harmondsworth: Penguin, 1971).
6 H. Harlow, 'Love in infant monkeys' reprinted in T. Eisner and E. O. Wilson (eds.), *Animal Behaviour, readings from the Scientific American* (San Francisco, W. H. Freeman and Company, 1975) p. 254.
7 Quoted in I. Stickland, *The Voices of Children 1700–1914*, pp. 76, 78.
8 Charles Lamb, 'Witches and other night fears' in *Essays of Elia* (London: Dent, 1915) pp. 109–10.
9 E. Jones, preface to P. M. Pickard, *I Could a Tale Unfold* (London: Tavistock Publications, 1961) p. ix.
10 P. Thompson, 'Voices from within' in H. J. Dyos and M. Wolff (eds.), *The Victorian City, images and reality* (London: Routledge, 1973) p. 60.
11 L. de Mause (ed.), *The History of Childhood* p. 127.
12 G. O. Trevelyan, *Life and Letters of Lord Macaulay*, pp. 41–3.
13 H. Harlow, 'Love in infant monkeys'.
14 R. Benedict, 'Continuities and discontinuities,' pp. 22–3.
15 A. Macfarlane, *The Family Life of Ralph Josselin* (Cambridge: Cambridge University Press, 1970) p. 90.
16 R. W. White, 'Competence and the psycho-sexual stages of development' in R. S. Lazarus and E. M. Opton (eds.), *Personality: selected readings* (Harmondsworth: Penguin, 1967) pp. 142–66.

4. THE CHILD'S MIND

1 W. James, *The Principles of Psychology*, vol. 1 (London: Macmillan, 1890) p. 488.

2 K. Chukovsky, *From Two to Five*, trans. M. Morton (Berkeley: University of California Press, 1966) p. 38.

3 N. Isaacs, quoted in S. Isaacs *Intellectual Growth in Young Children* (London: Routledge, 1930) p. 108.

4 G. Jahoda, 'Child animism: a critical survey of cross-cultural research,' *Journal of Social Psychology*, 1958, 47, pp. 197–222.

5 G. Jahoda, 'The development of children's ideas about country and nationality,' *British Journal of Educational Psychology*, 1963, 33, pp. 47–60.

6 R. Firth, *Human Types* (New York: Mentor Books, 1958) p. 122.

7 M. Douglas, *Purity and Danger* (London: Routledge, 1966) p.58.

8 J. Piaget, *Play, Dreams and Imitation in Childhood* (London: Routledge, 1951) p. 198.

9 See P. Burke, *A New Kind of History: from the writings of Febvre* (London: Routledge, 1973) p. xiv.

10 K. Thomas, *Religion and the Decline of Magic* (London: Weidenfeld and Nicolson, 1971).

11 A. M. Shearman, quoted in the *Guardian*, 8 September 1971.

12 G. Gorer, *Exploring English Character* (London, Cresset Press, 1955) p. 269.

13 R. Firth, *Human Types*, p. 123.

14 M. Douglas, *Purity and Danger*, p. 78.

15 J. S. Bruner, *The Relevance of Education* (London, Allen and Unwin, 1972) p. 13.

16 See J. H. Flavell, *The Developmental Psychology of Jean Piaget* (New York: Van Nostrand, 1963) p. 331.

17 See B. Lloyd, *Perception and Cognition* (Harmondsworth: Penguin, 1972) pp. 133–4.

18 D. Elkind, *Children and Adolescents: interpretative essays on Jean Piaget* (New York: Oxford University Press, 1970) p. 21.

19 J. M. Tanner, *Education and Physical Growth* (London: University of London Press, 1961) p. 85.

20 See J. H. Flavell, *The Developmental Psychology of Jean Piaget*, p. 373.

21 Quoted in I. Pinchbeck and M. Hewitt, *Children in British Society* (London: Routledge, 1973) p. 351.

22 Quoted in P. Ariès, *Centuries of Childhood*, p. 128.

23 M. Weir, *Shoes were for Sunday* (London: Hutchinson, 1970) p. 16.

24 See, for example, P. Bryant, *Perception and Understanding in Young Children* (London: Methuen, 1974).

25 Quoted in M. King-Hall, *The Story of the Nursery* (London: Routledge, 1958) p. 154.

26 J. S. Bruner, *The Relevance of Education*, pp. 27–30.

5. SUMMING UP: WHAT IS A CHILD?

1 O. Lewis, *La Vida* (London: Panther, 1968) p. 53.
2 See U. Bronfenbrenner, *Two Worlds of Childhood* (Harmondsworth: Penguin, 1974).
3 P. Thompson, 'The war with adults,' p. 30.
4 J. Piaget, *Science of Education and the Psychology of the Child* (New York: Orion Press, 1970) p. 153.
5 Quoted in R. A. Durr, *On the Mystical Poetry of Henry Vaughan* (Cambridge, Mass.: Harvard University Press, 1962) pp. 13–14.
6 J. H. van den Berg, *The Changing Nature of Man* (New York: Dell, 1961) p. 28.
7 J. B. Hill (ed.), *Boswell's Life of Johnson* (Oxford: Clarendon Press, 1934), Vol. II, pp. 407–8.
8 J. H. van den Berg, *The Changing Nature of Man*, pp. 29–30.
9 W. S. Stoner, *Manual of Natural Education* (Indianapolis: Bobbs-Merill Company, 1916) p. 16.
10 M. Deakin, *The Children on the Hill* (London: André Deutsch, 1972).
11 J. S. Bruner, *The Relevance of Education*, pp. 50-1.
12 J. B. Watson, *Behaviourism* (USA: People's Publishing Company, 1925) p. 104.
13 J. Piaget, *Science of Education and the Psychology of the Child*, p. 153.

Suggested
further reading

PHILIPPE ARIÈS, *Centuries of Childhood* (London: Jonathan Cape, 1962).
  This is certainly the most stimulating book on the history of childhood so far written. By tracing attitudes towards the child in France from medieval times to the modern family, Ariès argues that our whole concept of childhood today is a modern invention, and something that would be quite unrecognizable five hundred years ago.

PETER COVENEY, *The Image of Childhood* (Harmondsworth: Penguin, 1967).
  The author describes here some of the ways in which children have been portrayed in literature, from the romantic images of childhood in Blake and Wordsworth to the different views of twentieth-century authors, later influenced by psychoanalytic theory. The contrasting images of childhood that result are useful reminders of the relative nature of childhood, as seen from very different viewpoints.

RUTH BENEDICT, *Patterns of Culture* (London: Routledge, 1935).
  One of the first and most influential anthropological works that set out to demonstrate that children – and indeed all mankind – are very much the products of particular cultures and societies. It contains, among other things, a powerful warning against studying individual characteristics regardless of their possible social significance and background.

MARGARET MEAD and MARTHA WOLFENSTEIN (eds.), *Childhood in Contemporary Cultures* (Chicago: University of Chicago Press, 1955).
  This is a stimulating collection of essays edited by two of the foremost researchers into different aspects of child behaviour in particular cultures. Margaret Mead has also written two classic works around this theme, based on her own research in the field: *Growing Up in New Guinea* and *Coming of Age in Samoa*.

URIE BRONFENBRENNER, *Two Worlds of Childhood, USA and USSR* (Harmondsworth: Penguin, 1970).

In this book, a psychologist looks at the different ways of bringing up children current in the USA and the USSR Such variations in parental response and educational practice, Bronfenbrenner claims, are themselves responsible for many of the different habits and norms found when the children of these two continents are compared, not always to America's advantage. A stimulating, sometimes disturbing work.

WILLIAM KESSEN, *The Child* (New York: Wiley, 1965).

This volume usefully edits some of the most important psychological contributions towards different concepts of the child, from the first, enormously influential statements of Rousseau through to the work of Freud and Piaget. The selection and accompanying notes should be helpful to non-psychologists who may find some of the originals too complex.

ERIK ERIKSON, *Childhood and Society* (New York: Norton, 1950).

Drawing on psychoanalytic theory, Erikson presents here his own view of human development, starting with the baby and continuing to old age. Erikson's important modifications to Freudian theory, and in particular his stress upon social aspects of development, have been widely welcomed. This book has been especially influential.

JEROME BRUNER, *The Relevance of Education* (London: Allen and Unwin, 1972).

These essays, by one of the foremost contemporary psychologists, concentrate upon the growth of intellect in the child and in particular on how he perceives the world around him. Broadly sympathetic to Piaget's theories, all Bruner's work on children's cognitive growth is interesting, but these essays are a good introduction to more complex material.

Subject index

Index of names